A FIGHTER'S PURPOSE: OVERCOMING THE BATTLE WITHIN

BY KIMBERLY ROSE

A Fighter's Purpose: Overcoming the Battle Within

Trilogy Christian Publishers A Wholly Owned Subsidiary of Trinity Broadcasting Network

2442 Michelle Drive Tustin, CA 92780

Copyright © 2022 by Kimberly Rose

Scripture quotations marked NIV are taken from the Holy Bible, New International Version®, NIV®. Copyright © 1973, 1978, 1984, 2011 by Biblica, Inc.TM Used by permission of Zondervan. All rights reserved worldwide. www.zondervan.com. The "NIV" and "New International Version" are trademarks registered in the United States Patent and Trademark Office by Biblica, Inc.TM.

No part of this book may be reproduced, stored in a retrieval system, or transmitted by any means without written permission from the author. All rights reserved. Printed in the USA.

Rights Department, 2442 Michelle Drive, Tustin, CA 92780.

Trilogy Christian Publishing/TBN and colophon are trademarks of Trinity Broadcasting Network.

Cover Photo © 2008 Dave Mandel

For information about special discounts for bulk purchases, please contact Trilogy Christian Publishing.

Trilogy Disclaimer: The views and content expressed in this book are those of the author and may not necessarily reflect the views and doctrine of Trilogy Christian Publishing or the Trinity Broadcasting Network.

Manufactured in the United States of America

10 9 8 7 6 5 4 3 2 1

Library of Congress Cataloging-in-Publication Data is available.

ISBN: 978-1-68556-502-2

E-ISBN: 978-1-68556-503-9

Dedication

This book is dedicated to those who suffer from mental struggles; it is not disability but ability. God doesn't want you to focus on what you cannot do but to focus on what you can do!

I would not have succeeded without the support of my husband, James Martin. Thank you for loving "all of me." Mom and Dad for always encouraging me and being in my corner, my siblings: Christy and her husband, Gary, for your listening ear; Bobby and his wife, Val, for your advice; and Kelley and her husband, Randy, for your twin power and support. To my stepchildren, thank you for giving me the gift of experiencing a piece of motherhood. To my nephews Brett, Matthew, Kayden, Bryce, and Liam: never give up pursuing your dreams; and to all my coaches and mentors who inspired me to be the best I could be.

I thank God for the mountaintops and valleys, the wins and the losses, the victories and defeats. Without you, I am nothing, and with you, I am everything.

—In loving memory of Ada Dilley

"Now to him who is able to do immeasurably more than all we ask or imagine, according to his power that is at work within us, to him be glory in the church and in Christ Jesus throughout all generations, for ever and ever! Amen."

Ephesians 3:20-21 (NIV)

Chapter 1

"He says, 'Be still, and know that I am God.'"

Psalm 46:10 (NIV)

I was seeking a change for my life, I wanted to go and experience the world on a mission trip, and this surprisingly led me to Impact 195, which was a yearlong discipleship program designed to experience Christian community, learn your identity in Christ, and essentially sit at the feet of Jesus for just about nine months. I was hooked. I remember having so much hope through this program. Maybe I will meet my husband; maybe I will go on my first mission trip. I couldn't wait to see what God had in store. I was working as a paramedic at the time, and I had been one for about twelve years or so. And I was working with San Diego Fire Department and Rural metro. I was working nights during this time, so it would allow me to attend the program.

After a lot of class teachings service projects that would include helping the elderly with house chores like changing the smoke detector and cleaning or picking up trash, I was creating a lot of memories with my new Impact community. It was time to embark on my first mission trip. I was thirty-one years old, and I wanted to experience firsthand what it would be like to travel out of the country and not only for my selfish purposes but do it in the name of the Lord! Where would it be? I have heartstrings attached to Asia. I had dreams as a child to go to the Serengeti. Well, it turned out to me having some options: the two teams were traveling to Haiti and to Africa. My heart yearned for Africa. Guinea, Africa it was! There weren't lions or zebras gallivanting on the plains of the Serengeti, but it was a country that desperately needed the Lord. We were to travel and host a pastors' conference to share with the surrounding communities. Each one of us would choose a topic to give a twenty-minute or so presentation. I always had a deep impact on spiritual prayer, and I chose that to be my topic. We would also be doing a medical outreach to the community in a clinic and sharing the love of Jesus through an orphanage visit. There was also one more service project. To visit an African prison and medical ward encouraging and bringing the miracle hope of Jesus and healing to a place of isolation, loneliness, and sickness.

I was on my way! Ready to see the amazing workings of Jesus. Faith-filled, motivated, and inspired. We traveled with a small team to explore Guinea. I was there for ten days. And of course, had to get all my shots up to date and was prescribed Malarone to take, which is an anti-malaria drug. Little did I know this would change the trajectory of my life forever.

Africa was amazing. I remember stepping into the convention center and meeting a ton of pastors from around Africa there to soak up every word and worship unto the Lord. These people traveled hundreds of miles and some on the back of trucks. We stayed in a small compound that felt safe, didn't have a legit address, but it was safe enough for me. Guinea was having some political unrest during

Chapter 1

our visit with new elections that were going on. I remember traveling down the streets and seeing protests that were going on and people throwing rocks! Our leaders were trying to minimize it, but when I look back on it now, it was a situation to be concerned about. I met a team of prayer warriors. Women that knew their scripture, tenacious, and did I say intimidating? I was supposed to teach them about prayer, and let me tell you, they could teach me far more. I had a translator for the talk, and it went well. I used some visual props and brought my fighting gloves; I started to punch at a person's hand to demonstrate fighting back at Satan. I wasn't sure what they thought about that. Part of my history was being a professional MMA fighter, but I will go into that later.

We continued on with the trip, had a medical outreach, and a young woman came up to me who was pregnant; she looked to be close to nine months, and she was having stomach pains. My friend Sheryl and I prayed for her, and instead of taking the anti-biotics the local doctor gave her, I instructed her to take the salt tablets to help with dehydration and have been feeling a sense from the Lord to have her rest. I gave her a book that I brought on Psalm 23 about resting. I later gave another gift to my translator and learned that the young woman was his pregnant wife! God had already placed it on my heart to add to the gifts by bringing the book, and it blessed her. The next day she was pain-free, and we gave glory to God.

We went to the prison, and that was quite a somber place, literally hundreds of men, malnourished, crammed together in a tiny cell. We would share the news of the gospel and offer salvation. I remember the first time I shared the gospel, I broke down and cried, sharing it with the prison medical ward. I felt loneliness and depression there and was moved with compassion to share the Love of Jesus, that they didn't have to die alone. There was a God who understood them and would save them, a God that wanted to have a real relationship with them full of forgiveness and truth.

Africa was an amazing experience, and if I were to recall one thing that blew my mind was their ability to worship our King of kings. I remember lying in bed at night at the compound, and at two in the morning, I would hear an African acapella-style singing coming from the common room. It was as if heaven opened up, and they were singing. We also would have a celebration of dancing and singing after every session at the pastors' conference. It was explosive, dynamic, filled with passion. I literally felt the earth shake with Joy for our Lord and worshipping with the African culture.

It was time for an end to our amazing trip. I received a special anointed blessing from one of the elderly women in the prayer group and was on my way home to share the wonderous working God did on my first mission trip.

Things were getting back to normal; I was elated from the trip. People in my discipleship group would say I had the Holy Spirit upon me when I came back. I finished my rounds of my Malarone medication about a week or so after I got back, and that's when things started to shift.

I felt clearer, more in tune with the Lord, sensing His direction and following His voice. I was still working nights and adjusting to

Chapter 1

the time change. I started to grow deeper and deeper into what now I know is called *"mania."*

It started rather slowly; I began to have some in-depth delusions. Most of them were spiritual. The difficult thing about this is that I remember all of them. Some were embarrassing, some made sense in a weird kind of way. But more importantly, this was the beginning of a diagnosis that I still can ultimately say I still have a hard time with.

I remember having an attraction to a man that was involved in my community. I literally thought that we were married spiritually and somehow had this quiet connection. I did the strangest things, brought him food the next day, wrote in a journal daily about our connection in hopes of it being a document of our love story. I would get up in the early morning of the night and pray deeply for him and the people in our immediate community. I am blessed and grateful that through all the confusion and illness, this person respected my dignity and kept a lot of this confidential in what a public display I was showing. He was being a true brother in Christ, protecting me.

The night that it all unfolded, I thought I was going to my wedding ceremony. It was at the cliffs in OB San Diego. I was standing there in silence, stillness, imagining an intricate story in my mind. I even had a police officer approach me because someone called and was concerned I wasn't moving. I told him I was fine; I was still halfway in this world too. He left me alone and thought I was just meditating at the beach. It was a night that I stayed up all night. The early morning hours approached, and I was ready to go to the first church service.

I felt elated during worship; it was 8 a.m. and felt like this was where I was supposed to be. The first service came and went, and I felt directed by God to stay for the second one. Only this time, I felt that I should stand up in the middle of service with my hand outstretched and be still. This was when I experienced catatonia. The pastor just went along his business and preached his sermon. I am thankful today that he didn't cause a scene even though I was causing one for myself in the front row. I recall people moving away from me; some came up to me and touched and prayed for me. I was completely out of it. I still can't believe I stood up there still for more than an hour. The service ended, and that was when the staff was more concerned because I still was not moving. They called 911. To my dismay, I do remember that it was my old EMT partner that came to help. Unfortunately, I knew everybody that would come to my aid because I was a paramedic in the city for so many years.

I was transported by ambulance to the emergency room and explained that I had been on a recent trip to Africa and was taking Malarone, my anti-malaria pill. I came to the ER, and the doctor couldn't explain my abnormal behavior. I have no history of psych behavior or any signs of infection. They let me go as I signed out AMA. Against medical advice. I was not a threat to others or myself, so I was in my legal right.

My family, on the other hand, was very concerned as I hadn't had any medical problems growing up. And this was very alarming for

Chapter 1

them. The days following were not extreme catatonic behavior, but that included me purging, cleaning, and on an extreme diet. I felt as though I had to purge myself of toxins, wear certain colors, only wear purple sometimes because that was a wife of noble character in the Bible, clothed in purple. I would eat gluten-free, sugar-free, and cover my face sometimes in the face of evil. It was all very bizarre, but looking back, I can kind of see a little common sense to it. There was a disruption in my neurotransmitters, my biochemistry was haywire, and my body was doing anything and everything it could to correct and balance out the situation.

My parents had taken off for the weekend, and though I was showing some progress, I had seen a psychiatrist who believed that my psychosis was from the Malarone and a low dose of anti-psychotic should help correct it. I was placed on a low dose. I was by myself and decided to clean my parents' house from top to bottom to rid myself of evil influences. Lucky for me, there wasn't a fire because I was spraying cleaner around a lit fireplace. My parents got wind of something wrong and came home. I had a full-on panic attack and was anxious, distraught, and worried I was going to die. They took me back to the emergency room. I was becoming catatonic again, and I received smelling salt and an IM injection of Geodon. I remember being groggy and tired.

My next stop was in the mental hospital. I was scared out of my mind; I felt like people were out to get me. And nothing is scarier when you are in a hospital with other people who are not sane themselves. It was a time of continued prayer, side effects from new medication being introduced, and separation from my family and loved ones. I was diagnosed with bipolar disorder.

Bipolar is a chemical imbalance in the brain; it is not widely understood, but to my understanding, my neurotransmitters are out of whack. There are times of depression, and there is hypomanic, which is just elated feelings, intense focus, not a whole lot of need for sleep. And mania that I had experienced was delusions of grandeur and a whole lot of abnormal behavior. There is type 2 bipolar, which can be treated with medication but not progress to type 1, which requires hospitalization. I had never experienced depression or suicidal thoughts till this day, but I think the depression side goes into more of just being tired for me and having general fatigue.

Coming face to face with that diagnosis was and is the hardest thing I will go through; not only have I gone through public humiliation from being manic, but now I have a lifetime illness that I daily fight shame with and have to be on medication for the rest of my life. Not an easy thing to face at thirty-two years old.

I recall a psychiatric patient I transported once as a paramedic, and her statement deeply resonates with me until this day. She went on to say that everyone is fearful of the mentally ill, what they will do, what they will say if they will harm someone. But it is the ill that is truly terrified. Fearful that someone will harm us, fearful in facing what is real and what is false. I will always remember that I was the one truly terrified in the hospital. I had been a dedicated Christian since I was eighteen years old. I was hurt that I had heard God incorrectly, I felt deceived, I didn't know how to hear His voice, would I ever be

Chapter 1

able to correctly be guided by His voice again? All these questions have been answered in the years to come, and it's been a long close abiding relationship with the Lord as He was the only one to truly understand in the stillness of night, in the cold hospital bed, in my thoughts what His love for me was.

I can narrow it down to two different incidents that occurred with my parents when I was sick. One time I just surrendered, crawled up into my mother's arms and cried like a baby. She was a retired LVN psych nurse, so to my benefit, she never was fearful of me, scared, or didn't know how to react. Of course, she was a loving mother, but at that moment, I remember just being held with love as I cried. Another was with my father; the hospital or mental ward had gardens on the patio. And I was too medicated to talk, so my father and I would just sit in the garden, not talking but being present. It never felt awkward or unloving, like there wasn't a whole lot to say; it was more of "I am here with you, present with you, loving you, and will see you through this." It was this moment that I understood sometimes with the Lord, you don't understand why things are happening, He may not give you answers. But to be still with Him and know that He is God as in Psalm 46:10.

I was discharged from the hospital with three months to rest, heal and adjust to my medication. I had moved back home to my parents and would enter a season of change. So many questions. What would my future be like as a bipolar? Was I even really bipolar? How do I move on? I haven't been hospitalized since then, but I have had some close calls, but I can honestly say I never want to be in that distress again. God has given me an amazing supportive family during this time. Only a few friends. But God was my Savior, and all I have is Him to trust in.

Chapter 2

"I know what it is to be in need, and I know what it is to have plenty."

Philippians 4:12 (NIV)

Rewind a few years back, and the scripture above would hold true; I truly knew what it felt like to be at the top of my life and what it felt to be at the lowest in my life.

I had just gotten over a bad heartbreak; my boyfriend of three and a half years ended our relationship. I was devastated. We were playing soccer together on Friday nights, and now that we were done, the team was done too. I had been spending the day with my twin sister, and we got frozen yogurt. We were walking around Poway, and I saw a sign that read "Poway Boxing Club." I urged her to go in and see what the place was all about.

I walked in, still eating my yogurt, and talked to one of the owners. I asked about classes, prices, and a more important question: when would I be able to compete? When would I be able to fight? She stated maybe in a year or so if I trained hard. I was intrigued. I asked if they had Friday evening classes available since my schedule seemed to have cleared up.

I remember walking into the gym. A ring stood in the corner; it was small, the people were nice, and I met the instructor Donnie. He was a professional boxer and pretty much had to wrap my hands for me since I knew nothing. I was hooked. With music from Rocky playing in the background, my heart just healed, and I cried at the same time with every punch I threw into the bag. It was like an emotional outlet I had never experienced before. I wanted to pursue more; after learning how to correctly throw a jab, straight right, and a left hook, I moved up in the boxing gym world and decided I wanted to spar. Getting in the ring was invigorating. I was nervous, I had headgear, my mouthpiece, and gear to protect my stomach. There were a few women who didn't mind sparring. I had another male friend that had already fought a smoker fight which is basically an exhibition match just for fun. He was super tall, super strong, and I think now looking back, he was the only person to have hit me, and I saw little stars or flashes of light, maybe because I was a sitting duck, not defending myself probably that well. But I was nervous every time I sparred with him. Donnie would get in the ring with me, and I think that was the best because, as a professional trainer, he knew how to push me and when to back off. I was a little overweight but had always been athletically inclined despite my extra curves. It was time to take this to the next step. It was time to train for my first fight!

I had been in the gym only three months, and my first smoker fight had approached. I had new boxing shoes, boxing shorts; I was ready. We had the event at the boxing club in Carlsbad. My whole family showed up; there was a packed audience. I didn't know much about my opponent other than she had come from a different gym. The show was getting ready to start. Just one problem: the commission who regulated the safety for the event required there to be a paramedic on hand in case someone got hurt. They were going to cancel the event. It just so happened that I, of course, work as a

Chapter 2

paramedic, and the company that I work for did special events. I was talking with a department brother of mine and explained the situation. It must have been an answered prayer because he somehow arranged to pick up the ambulance, pick up the narcotics, and head down to Carlsbad to save the day! DC was a brother in Christ in my life, and he made my first fight happen.

I remember a lot that night, but one thing I remember specifically is a small voice in my head that told me, *You better start getting used to this. You better start getting used to the crowd.* I will never forget that saying. The bell rang, and I think we must have punched a hundred times a minute. We fought three two-minute rounds. Which, in the big picture, isn't much, but when you are new and you are non-stop punching, your lungs get tired as they have never gotten tired before. I remember all the cheering, being up against the ropes and at the end of the match, standing there with my opponent. I was ecstatic. I have always been a good sport and showed professionalism and care for my opponent. They declared the match a tie. Though I would have liked to have had the win for my first fight, I was honored to share with her a big trophy which we each got. I loved all the support I got from my family, from my gym, and from people I didn't even know.

I was stoked about my first fight and wanted to keep pushing forward. Donnie, unfortunately, was leaving the gym, and I didn't have anyone to train me to go further. My next step was amateur. I was twenty-seven years old. Never put on boxing gloves in my life, and this opened amazing opportunities.

I was on the search for a new gym, a new coach. It was then I found city boxing located in downtown San Diego. I made the drive to pursue my goal as an amateur boxer. The gym was rugged. I felt like a fighter. I felt inspired they had a huge ring to train in and tons of people who looked to take this seriously. I first then met Larry, who taught the evening classes. He taught me how to wrap my hands in a way that I still do to this day. I would work hard, keep my nose down, stay humble, and put the word out that I was looking for a coach. I met my first female professional boxer, Kristy. She had an amazing record and was coached by a man named Carlos. He was an old-school Mexican boxing coach and had a small team that he trained and did mitts in the middle of the ring. I remember when he first called me up to train. He never was officially employed there, but I ended up being under his team. There were four of us at the time. Kristy, getting ready for a pro fight, Ryan, another amateur boxer that wanted to go pro, would never stop staring at himself in the mirror making fight poses, and Marie, a younger girl with desires to train. We would meet every day. I started to take a weight cut a little more seriously. I even dabbled into a little kickboxing to increase my endurance. But boxing it was! I was training hard, sparring hard with other girls in the gym. It felt like a fight every time I sparred except for when I was sparring with my team. Even then, there was heavy pride. There is an art to being strong and a champion in the ring but still stay humble and respectful. That's the type of fighter I wanted to be, but like I said, I still wanted to be champion, and you still have an opponent who wants to hurt you and win, and you must step up and fight.

Chapter 2

I was ready for my first amateur fight. Unfortunately, it was with one of my sparring partners from another gym. I had been doing well against her sparring and thought I wouldn't have a problem in the ring. I didn't necessarily like that she was my opponent because we had already been studying each other. The first amateur fight was in a small gym. I had my protective gear, and I am laughing as I am writing this, but I had a chest protector. Apparently, it was optional. But as we were fighting, my chest cup popped out of my shirt and landed in the middle of the ring. They had to stop the fight due to the disruption and pick it up. I remember not knowing what to do. Do I put it back? The ref was looking at me like she wasn't going to do it; my hands were in my gloves. I think eventually, the ref ended up helping a sister out. But later found out that I didn't even need it. Needless to say, that would be the last time I would use a chest cup. The match went well. We used ten-ounce gloves, which were smaller, and I was more concerned that they would hurt more. I remember feeling the punches stronger, but it was something I could handle. I ended up losing. I was really bummed; I even cried. My coach Carlos would say that I had won the fight, but the judges saw things differently. I would not give up but reevaluate and look on to my next match.

It was time for Coachella, a huge boxing tournament. I wanted to enter the bigger fights, but you need five fights under your belt to go for Nationals. It was time to step in the ring again. I had never seen such a big tournament. I was just coming off from my loss and still getting my feet wet. I remember not making a big cut in weight for the fight; I believe it was at 155. I was getting nervous. We were waiting around forever. And I was eating these energy goo packets that were making me wired. My coach told me to go sit down because I was getting all weird. I remember before the fight, he taught me one simple move. To just duck when she punched because she was much taller than I was. Her name was Nicole, and she was cocky with a loud annoying family with her on the sidelines. My team and her team started to get into it as well. I was getting super nervous and was praying to God for a sign if I should fight. I was self-doubting myself. I got my hands wrapped and went up to an official to have him sign them off. He stated, "You're in luck; everyone who has had their hands checked by me has won tonight." I knew that I was meant to fight. I knew that victory could be mine. The fight began, and the darndest thing happened. I just began to do a simple duck when she punched. It slipped right by. Then I would exchange my punches, and the fight was simple. The final announcement came after the judges scored the bout. My hand was raised. It was my first tournament win, and a great big belt came along with it. I will never forget my firsthand raised. The official I saw afterward said, "See, I said you would win." My signs from God had been sealed.

I was coming down from my high of winning my first belt, and I felt like I still had a lot of work to do. My next matches were to gain up my five, so I could enter National PAL. I fought a lot at Westminster boxing gym in LA. This older fellow helped set up fights for me. Some I lost, and they never wanted to rematch me probably because I hit so hard, and I even went to Las Vegas for an amateur bought. This girl looked in shape and had a mean demeanor. Even my family thought she would beat me by the looks of it. The bell rang, and our exchanges were tough. My hits were harder, and she began to retreat from me in the ring. I won that fight, too, even though later I am pretty sure my nose got a little broken. I think it might have got chipped because I had the typical watering of the eyes and swelling. I was a real boxer now!

It was time for National Pal, which stood for police athletic commission. If I won this fight, it would sponsor me to USA Nationals. I had my parents in the audience, and this fight you can find on Youtube. I fought Trina. I had worked a lot on my movement, and you can tell I was in and out with my exchanges. At one point, I was backing her up, and I dropped her with a punch. I couldn't believe I had dropped a girl with us wearing headgear. They evaluated her face because I believe her nose started to bleed. They stopped the fight. My first technical knockout, I suppose. I won another belt, and next was USA Nationals for me.

I started to talk and meet with many different people, and I was online talking to a professional MMA fighter. We talked about the profession, and I expressed an interest in training. He invited me to the gym he taught at called Knockout Fitness. This gym was by far my favorite. I immediately gained a connection training with Dave and met the team from Deth Ko Sin. It was here I was introduced to Muay Thai and my master trainer Kru Mark. Now he was an older Kru, and the motivation and inspiration he taught were amazing. I started to take classes and remember how hard I trained. I wanted to please him as a student. I wanted to please him as a person with passion. Both Carlos and Kru Mark were father figures to me. I looked up to them to direct me and guide me in this fighting world. I knew it wasn't going to be easy, but I had to talk to Carlos and let him know I was training in MMA and Jiu-Jitsu.

The conversation with Carlos didn't go very well. He pretty much discouraged me and told me I would never amount to anything; I wasn't a good fighter, and I just hit hard. That really hurt me, but I knew where I ultimately wanted to go was professional, and it wasn't in boxing. I had a very important decision to make. Pursue boxing and possibly be the first female in the Olympics or become a professional MMA fighter.

I still had to go to USA Nationals, and this time I would be taking one of my coaches, Dave, to coach me. He wasn't a boxer, but he was a fighter, and I had faith we would do well. It was held in the Olympic training center in Colorado Springs. So, feeling confident in my sponsored sweatsuit, I headed to Colorado to get acclimated to the elevation. I would be fighting at 138. My first fight was easy, I had the upper hand the whole time, and Dave told me that if I was behind in points, that meant to bite down and swing away. I had won my first match. It was time for the second, and this one was to go to the finals. My opponent had a bye the first day, so she was a lot more refreshed. The match began, and she was super wild and consistent. My jab was jabbing away, only to my surprise, they were not counting it. Only the punches with the shoulder torqued back would count. My coach said to swing away. I was exhausted from my previous fight the day before, and it wasn't enough. Even with her wild and sloppy punches, I had lost the match but won a bronze medal in the tournament. It discouraged me to see her move on to the finals to fight Queen, who later became one of the first females to fight in the Olympics in Beijing. I would have loved to test myself against a great fighter. She ended up winning US Nationals, and that was a wrap. I would go home with my bronze, ready to lay down my ten-ounce gloves to pick up my four-ounce ones in pursuit of a professional MMA career.

I had to train a lot in Muay Thai; I think I would literally stay in late on weekends to practice my kicks. I would do hundreds of them. I always reminded myself of the scripture to be faithful with few things, and I will be blessed with greater. I knew that the hard work that I did when no one was looking would be honored in public. I had my first Muay Thai fight at Song Kran festival in Thai town, Los Angeles. I was honored and learned Kru Mark's Wai Kru. This is a ceremonial dance fighters do before the fight to honor their Kru. I was wearing Kru Mark's Rose, Mongok, which is a Thai ceremonial headpiece and a leigh of flowers. It was to be the most honorable fight because it was in the Thai community. Song Kran is the Thais new year festival. It was super-hot, and I went over the top rope, which signifies confidence. My opponent probably was nervous because I was a last-minute addition to the matches, and here, I was doing the ancient ceremonial dance, the Wai Kru. During the dance, you aim at your opponent with an arrow that signifies an important lesson Kru Mark taught me, the basis for his family fight style. No matter what, keep moving forward like an arrow. The fight was a little hectic because they were spraying the mats with water since it was so hot out, and I kept slipping when I would throw a kick. But more importantly, I kept moving forward like an arrow. I loved fighting to the Thai music, and this match would ultimately lead into a tie. I honored my opponent and was honored to fight for Deth Ko Sin in my first Muay Thai fight.

***

Next stop was amateur MMA. My coach Dave had connections with TUFFNUFF, which was an amateur MMA company that did matches in Las Vegas. I had a couple of fights offered for my first one, but finally, one came. It would be at the Tropicana Hotel Las Vegas. Now to the important part. What song would be my entrance song? I chose "So Far Away" by Stained. I got my hair braided; I had my MMA shorts printed with DKS logo. And more important, my nickname came about on my shorts, "Little Pit Bull." Now I know this is cliché, but there is a story behind my nickname. I was reading the book *A Fighter's Heart* by Sam Sheridan at the time, and in this book, they talked about pit bull dogfighting. They went on to say that the dogs that would cross the fighting line were loved and taken care of the most by their owners. They would fight harder, they would fight out of the love that they had been given; therefore, I was a little pit bull. I fought out of the love for God, my family, my coaches, my team. The fight was kind of wild for me. I was still a newbie at Jiu-Jitsu, so I didn't know quite what to expect if I was on the ground. I knew my fight game was standing. I would try and keep it. My opponent

Chapter 2

was Karina. I will never forget her or my first fight. In the end, they took a long time judging it, it was so close, and she was a great fighter. But I ended up getting my hand raised. I remember talking with her a whole lot while we were waiting for the results. And to this day, I consider her a friend. Little did I know there was someone particular in the audience that night who watched our fight, and I got the call of a lifetime three weeks later for my professional debut.

It was for Kim Couture, the famous champion Randy Couture's wife.

Wow! What an amazing offer! The money wasn't that great, but they were offering to pay for all my medical expenses, a 1,000 purse, and I would be fighting for a partnership event with ESPN at the Thomas & Mack arena in Las Vegas. It was a free night of boxing and MMA. I was ready more than ever. I knew that she had world championship coaches. Randy Couture and I are not 100 percent, but I think she had well-known fighters in her corner as well, watching her previous fights. I knew I could beat her. I had been dating a teammate at the time, and we ran into some complications with my coach Dave. I knew that this would be an amazing opportunity to get sponsors. I had three weeks to prepare. My coach and I were having a disagreement with obtaining sponsors. I am also saying that I wasn't the easiest person to get along with, to be honest. We also had a disagreement about who would be the head coach in the ring, I thought it should be Kru Mark, and he thought differently. With everything adding up, he ended up backing out of the match the last week. Kru Mark, who never corners his fighters, ended up cornering me. I had him, my boyfriend at the time, and Kru Mark's wife. Deth Ko Sin was ready to proclaim its name to the world.

I felt confident with my corner and went to Las Vegas. My whole family was headed there and some supportive friends. I got a few sponsors and some fighting gear. We stayed at Planet Hollywood for the weigh-ins, and I remember being interviewed, lots of cameras, and our face off. Kim seemed nice and even broke the ice a little bit when it was our turn. I met Randy and recalled Dave Matthew's band song "Where Are You Going" in the background. It was time for a good night's rest for a fight that would change my life forever.

It was fight day. I remember just relaxing all day and making my way to the arena. I was about to walk in and saw my family getting ready to enter. That was a blessing. The event was promoted by the Couture. I remember getting a gift basket in my hotel room with a thank you card and treats. I was brought in by them to lose. It was their promotion, their event. I was supposed to be Kim's first win. God had other plans. The promotion interviewed me before the fight; they asked me who my favorite fighter was and why. I said it was Muhammad Ali that he fought Ken Norton in 1973 and received a broken jaw in the second round and went on to fight ten rounds and won. What a precursor to what was about to happen. They never aired the video either. I am sitting in the underground hallway, listening to the crowd. Was I nervous? No, I had my own private warm-up room, I did the Wai Kru privately before my fight, and I was on my way to the ring. It was a ring instead of a cage because they had boxing matches earlier and still were allowed to technically have

Chapter 2

an MMA fight but just had to put another rope there to make it five. I heard my song start to play. It was Linkin Park's "What I've Done." This is another precursor to the years to come. The lyrics resonated so deeply within me. I walked my walk with confidence, went over the top rope, and was ready to fight the fight of my life. I heard her song start. It was "Pour Some Sugar on Me" by Def Leppard. I still think of the fight every time I hear the song, which is a lot. Her nickname was Sugar-Free. I think because she wasn't so nice.

They introduced us, which felt like forever. We touched gloves, and I was ready for the fight. Kru Mark told me right before the bell rang to throw an overhand right, he felt that she would be throwing a back roundhouse. That was the only thing in my mind. So, I threw the overhand right, not sure where it landed, but it dropped her, and I just followed through with hammer fist punches. Couture recovered, and the first round had her on top of me, not making much movement. I could feel the punches from the bottom. I attempted to put her in an armbar, but I felt my body lifting, I was afraid I would be dropped on my head, so I let go. Which realistically would have given me a better opportunity to sink it in more, but I was a beginner on the ground. The bell rang. These were five-minute rounds, so you could feel them. Kru Mark didn't give me a chair in the corner; he had me stand up and stretch my legs like a Thai fighter. I guess there was no resting for me.

The second round was a little bit of us on the ground, I just held her on top of me in full guard, and she was so tired she didn't make much progress. The ref would stand us up, and it was a dominating stand-up game from my aspect. I could hear coaches from around the ring strategically giving her advice, and my family was a bit farther away, so I could not hear them. My mom had to take an Ativan just to watch, and my dad squeezed my nephew as he was anticipating each round.

The third round came. I just kept my stand-up game strong. We ended up on the ground for the last minute or so, and I was losing my full guard, but there wasn't enough time for her to do anything, she was absolutely exhausted, and I could have gone on for many more rounds. I was just so excited to have completed my first professional fight. I supported my opponent and hugged her with good sportsmanship. I waited with anticipation for the judge's decision. I didn't know the outcome because she was a favored fighter. Would they give it to her? I felt like I had done well, but you never really know. The wait and then my hand was raised, Kim Rose, the Little Pit Bull winning with a unanimous decision. I thanked God, my family, and my fight team. It was one of the greatest moments in my life, all that hard work, having faith that this was where I was supposed to be. I couldn't wait to celebrate with everyone. I couldn't wait to eat, drink and be merry.

The news hit the public fast. I had broken Kim Couture's jaw in three places, and our Youtube video got a lot of popularity. I was not ecstatic the day after but concerned with her well-being. I know that we both sign away the risks when entering a fight, but it doesn't feel good to send someone to the hospital and have a life-changing event.

After the fight, I had interviews, my picture put in a magazine, and I was quite the mini-celebrity for a little while. It was hard for me to be in the limelight, so to speak, because I would read comments about the match, all were mostly good, and then I would read a bad one and get all hurt. I didn't have as thick of skin as I thought. I started to have some relationship problems with my boyfriend at the time, and I was pulled from my team. Knockout Fitness closed its doors as a gym, and I found myself isolated for a long time.

I tried to train with different gyms and coaches and even had some amazing fight offers after that. Some with Mejumi Fugi, Meisha Tate. I didn't feel ready on the ground. I didn't have confidence in my corner. And for some reason, it just didn't happen again. There was even a match at the local casino; my opponent backed out the night before, and they pulled someone off the street to fight me. I felt like that wasn't honorable. I wasn't a fighter who would fight anyone anytime, anywhere; I felt like a champion who should be a little more strategic in picking fights. I knew I was too early in the game to probably do that, but now looking back on it, I think it would have been honorable to even lose to some of the opponents I mentioned above. It just wasn't meant to be, and my momentum for competing stopped. I believe God wanted to focus on my identity being in Him and not an MMA fighter. I had placed what people thought of me above what He did and made it like an idol. It was all I could talk about, think about, and do. Being a professional fighter can be a lonely time as well; not a lot of people are putting the dedicated time into their training five hours a day which I did, and the ones who did, I wasn't feeling compatible to be a team. It was time to move on. There were other purposes God had in store from me. Sometimes we grip so tightly, holding on to the things we want when God just wants us to let go and receive His best plan for our lives.

I know how it feels now, reflecting on being at the top of my game and what it's like to be at the bottom, sick alone and not knowing who I was in Christ. This is something that I had years of developing. Do I still struggle with what people think of me? Yes, do I struggle with shame and guilt and trying to figure out my purpose for the Lord? I think it's a continuous refining process. But more importantly, my identity in Christ is the foundation of my being. Through the mountain peaks and the valleys below, God is the one who gives me meaning and loves me no matter what.

Chapter 3

*"Before I formed you in the womb I knew you,
before you were born I set you apart;
I appointed you as a prophet to the nations."*

Jeremiah 1:5 (NIV)

So I have been in a really confusing time. Here I had the top of my life, everyone loving me to becoming ill and basically isolating myself for a year. In the beginning, I felt some close friends would reach out to me, but others didn't know what to do. I think It was a combination of me pulling away and them just not knowing how to help. I felt like all the community I built in Impact was destroyed. I even remember me coming back from my hospital stay talking with the leaders and them pointing out it was all about Jesus and not to make it about me and put any idols in front of me. I was trying to place myself in an honest position of growth. What was it that I did to allow God to have this happen to me? How could I move forward?

I went back to the church for a Sunday service with my dad; somehow, I felt comfortable. I couldn't drive yet, and I recall being nervous in front of people. What would people think? Would anyone remember me from becoming catatonic? My friend Jen grabbed my hand and led me to the front with the school, who was getting prayer over, and everything went okay without incident.

God was encouraging me that it was safe to move forward from my trauma.

My personality was a little off. I was on anti-psychotic medication and lithium. I was asked a lot if I was okay, and my facial expressions were somber and downcast even though I was feeling fine inside.

This is where the healing would start, and my family was an intricate part in the healing process. Spending time with my nephews, taking them fishing, going to parks, and even if it was a movie. They were my best friends. They gave me hope and encouragement and didn't even think anything was wrong with me.

God knows our hurts and the traumatic things that we will go through. He set you apart in advance to do good things for Him. I remember a story my pastor once told. God is like a father well, He is our Heavenly Father, and in the way, a father is in a relationship with his child. It's like He is working on a project to build a bookshelf, and you are, let's say, three years old. He gives you a set of your play tools, and He has His grown-up tools. We know who really is going to build the bookshelf. He asks you to come alongside Him and help not for you to do it by yourself but so that He could have a relationship with you. I think too many times we take the credit for all the hard work, but it is truly God who enables and makes things happen.

So here I am, full of shame. I still struggle with it. What does shame look like to me and how does it make me feel or anybody, for that matter? I feel hidden, like I want to hide myself and my true feelings for worrying about what other people would think or say about me. It's true we must worry about what God thinks more than

Chapter 3

what people think. But oh so hard to do. I would also get very quiet and withdrawn. Not being myself around a group socially. I would have fear and worry for the future. It's like taking an inventory of everything that is wrong and carrying it as a burden on your back. It affects all relationships around you. Work, personal, family, friends. Whenever I think I have made a new milestone in my life, moving up professionally or relationally, I get a sense of freedom, and then a trigger happens. For me, it is rejection. I think the enemy also knows. Satan is real and wants to damage and ruin your relationship with Christ and with others. He would love for me to be isolated, shamed, and not bring the joy of the Lord to my life and those around it. We must set ourselves free in Christ to proclaim exactly what He wants to freely give us.

See, God is for you and not against you. He wants you to not only survive but to thrive. There are times of sadness and depression. Sometimes we just need to process our feelings and allow ourselves that process. We just don't want to get stuck there. One of my favorite stories in the Bible is that of Elijah, as in 1 Kings 19. He was a prophet. He was doing some amazing things for the Lord, and there was a woman named Jezebel that was after him and wanted to kill him. Elijah had some amazing prayers answered and a very close relationship with the Lord. One day it got overwhelming, so much that he just wanted to run away and die. It was a place in the Bible it ever talks about the feelings of suicide. Elijah did just that; he ran off into the wilderness and sat under a broom tree. "Jesus, take my life!" It was then an angel of the Lord approached him and said, "Get up and eat." So he did, went to sleep, and again the angel awoke him to eat, drink, rest and sleep. There was a long journey ahead. I feel like this was the scenario for my first year of healing. God just needed to care for me with the basics, nourish me on milk again before I would get to solid spiritual food. I think the best cure of all cures is a good night's sleep. It sets all your neurotransmitters back to balance, refreshes your spirit, and gets you clear-headed and ready for the next step. God is so gentle when He knows we are in over our heads or depressed enough to want to end it all. *He* takes care of the basics one step at a time; we just follow Him one step ahead.

I remember a saying if you were to climb a whole mountain all at once, you might feel overwhelmed at first if He were to show you the whole journey. Sometimes He puts a cloud at the top, so you just have to focus on the next step. Soon you will be making those step after step, and then before you know it, you reach the top.

Another powerful tool in becoming all God has created you to be is to be in His Word. And scripture memorization is amazing. Just when you may feel you're in a rut or you get a bad thought, a scripture you memorized earlier will divinely pop into your head. I think it's the clearest way God will speak to you. I personally use 2 Corinthians 10:4-5 (NIV) multiple times a day. "*The weapons we fight with are not the weapons of the world. On the contrary, they have divine power to demolish strongholds. We demolish arguments and every pretension that sets itself up against the knowledge of God, and we take captive every thought to make it obedient to Christ.*"

Chapter 3

I have some difficult thinking, sometimes called catastrophic thinking. I have spent so many years as a paramedic that death and dying have become a real part of my life. I have seen some families' worst nightmares, that car accident that took life too soon. Worry or fear can get the best of me. I always pray for safety, especially when I am driving home. I can't control everything that happens in my life, but I know the one who does. I must remind myself the odds of an accident are high. My family and I are not going anywhere without God saying so. And if some tragic circumstance happens, then I know it is in God's will. I thank and pray every day for the life He has given me. The people in it and what He is doing to constantly grow, shape, and mold me. Proverbs 3:5-6 (NIV) says, *"Trust in the Lord with all your heart and lean not on your own understanding; in all your ways submit to him, and he will make your paths straight."* In my darkest of times, God was there, these seasons don't last forever, times will change, and you never know what the tide will bring in, like in the famous movie quote *Castaway*.

Friendships have been a little difficult for me: I am an extroverted, outgoing person, but since getting sick, I have had an introverted part of me. I recently heard a sermon at church about cultivating friendships. A pastor went on to say casual friends are a product of your circumstances, whereas close friends are a matter of choice. You must be interested in others, not just interesting. If you live in Orange County, it's somewhat a rich neighborhood. There is a lot of entitlement going around. I have never felt that I had to keep up with the Joneses, but I have had lack of depth in forming new relationships.

I know it takes time. I have recently reconnected with a best friend from high school, and I joined her team briefly called Peppy Lime, using essential oils and natural products, which I will go into deeper later. I forgot how nice it is to have a community of girlfriends to talk things out. My husband is my best friend, but it's refreshing and good relationally to expand my inner circle again. I don't like forcing friendships, and I know it does hold true that you are the people you hang out with. But there are different levels of friends. You have your inner circle, friends from work, casual friends. My family is also like friends and has been there for me through everything. I have a twin sister, who is a paramedic also, an older sister, and an older brother who lives abroad. I think to have good friends, you need to be a good friend, and more importantly, when crisis time comes, and it always will. It's so important to be present. You may not have the best things to say or the wisest, but I can guarantee just to be there, present, nonjudgmental, will always mean more in the end.

I had a recent circumstance where I wasn't sure if it was my illness that led my new friends away or just a wrong perception of events. We joined a new small group, and after three-four weeks or so, I felt it was time to be vulnerable and open about my condition. After all, we are here to do life together and study God. I ended up sharing my testimony, and the very next day, this couple pulled from the group. Not only that, but they defriended me on Facebook. Now I know ultimately, it's their problem, and their behavior reflects them, but rejection is hard, and it still hurts. I have come to terms with it, and I truly pray for God to bring the right people into your life and remove

Chapter 3

the wrong ones. I would rather have found out earlier than later. I know writing this book will really make me feel vulnerable, but that's just it. I want to reach out to people who feel alone in their situation. We all struggle with these feelings, sick or not. I want to encourage those who are struggling with mental illness that they are not alone, there are challenges, but we can beat the odds. I believe those who are bipolar have an enormous ability to be creative and to tap into potential that sometimes regular people can't. There are plenty of famous people with mental illness. Winston Churchill, the prime minister of Britain, was one of the most famous leaders with bipolar. I love his quote: "*Success is not final, failure is not fatal: it is the courage to continue that counts.*"

***

It takes courage to battle mental illness. The ups and downs, the social stigma, if we come out of our shame and confusion. If we celebrate that which makes us unique, we will overcome. Other famous people who were known to suffer from the illness are Ernest Hemingway and also Vincent van Gogh, who painted some of the most amazing pictures during manic illness; Florence Nightingale, the first nurse, "the lady with the lamp," and Buzz Aldrin—they all suffered from mental illness. I believe through my own experiences that it is this gift given, yes, challenging at times, but it can be a form of inspiration, motivation, and ability to overcome and accomplish amazing tasks. I've been a paramedic, a professional fighter, a missionary, a wife, and a mom. I have done things in my life I would never have thought possible. I just had an ability to believe I could with God. There is no wisdom, no insight, no plan that can succeed against the Lord. If it is His will for you to accomplish something or be blessed with something, no one can ever take that away.

Chapter 4

"Whatever you do, work at it with all your heart, as working for the Lord, not for human masters."

Colossians 3:23 (NIV)

I was fifteen or so, fresh and ready to take on the world. The working world. My brother was a lifeguard for our community recreation center. He was the aquatic director. So he was in charge of who was hiring and who would teach swim lessons. My twin and I decided to follow in his footsteps and became AHA lifeguards and water safety instructors. I remember my interview with my brother. I was asked the question, "What if I would hire your sister over you?" I stated clearly that if she was the best person for the job and could save a life better than I could, then I would want you to hire her instead. My sister got asked the same question and her statement went on as something like, "Well, I would tell mom, and you would get into trouble." Well, we both ended up getting hired, so there was no trouble of the sort.

Becoming a pool lifeguard was great. Fun in the sun, teaching kids how to swim, even our annual slosh ball with some kegs of beer touched the limits of a blast. But it was one day that changed my life forever. It was a normal day, and I believe I was on a break. Suddenly, I heard a crash, there was a car accident right in front of the club. I went into action. I looked around with what I could bring to the scene to help. Mostly bandages, band-aids, and towels, I had nothing, or at least I couldn't think of anything to grab. I ran out to the accident. I didn't know what to do, was everyone okay? How am I supposed to help? Clearly, nobody is drowning. I heard sirens in the distance getting closer and closer. It was the paramedic ambulance. The medics got out of the ambulance with their equipment and went right to work organizing the scene. I just stood there and watched, enamored by their ability to help and control the scene. It was right then and there: I knew I wanted to become a paramedic. I think after all these years, it must be a calling. Well, I got that call from God that day.

I went on to graduate high school and immediately enrolled in EMT school to become an emergency medical technician. I had some struggles in school initially because I wasn't a good student in high school and had to kind of re-learn how to study in college. I remember I had to get a high grade on my final, and I had to start taking this class seriously if I wanted to pass. I got a great grade, and I was on my way to work for Balboa Ambulance. I have never worked retail or fast food. It was always emergency medicine, even if it was just first aid. I was born for this. Balboa was an interesting company, We did basic interfacility transports, basically taking the elderly to and from medical facilities, but occasionally we would get San Diego city 911 ringdown, which means when they are too busy and they would utilize other basic resources to help with the coverage, I responded to my first real emergency. Okay, so it wasn't too crazy, mostly falls and basic injuries. It was here I met my first

Chapter 4

real serious boyfriend, Kenny. We worked together. I would get all compassionate about the homeless people sleeping on the streets or passed out and wanted to stop to help them out. Well, in downtown San Diego I would be stopping to help a lot. After two years, I applied to the Palomar Community College paramedic program.

I was only twenty years old in school. I had to beat a lot of people out for the slots that were not sponsored by the fire department to get into the program. It was tough. We had simulations that were real-life scenarios created to test our protocol knowledge and ability to effectively assess and treat emergency patients. I was a little behind at first but started to get the hang of it. Trouble was I had no 911 emergency experience, only the basic ringdowns I was telling you about before. I had failed one simulation, and if I failed a second one, I was out of the program. I had two more simulations left, and they were all cardiac ones. How stressful! I was passing, and I got to my last simulation. We had a cardiac arrest. They were in ventricular tachycardia with a pulse on the monitor. I had a partner who was my radioman, and he also was instructed by me to shock the patient. When a person is in a lethal rhythm but still has a pulse, they are unstable and need a shock to the system, but there is a way to deliver this shock at the safest time of the heartbeat; it's called synchronized cardioversion. You press a button on the monitor, and it instructs the machine by delivering at just the right time. If a person was regularly shocked without rhyme or reason and had no regard as to the time, it would shock what is called defibrillation. My simulation partner ended up defibrillating my patient and not synchronizing it. I thought

I was done for sure. To my luck, they didn't hold my partner's action against me, and I moved on to clinical and field internships.

Downtown San Diego, medic unit 61, I was nervous for my first day. I showed up at fire station 1, super big and intimidating. My preceptor, Alan, was not, thank goodness. He was just about the most senior paramedic in San Diego, and I can remember the first time we met, he made me feel at ease, that we were in this together, and he was there to help get me through it. I had an amazing internship full of crazy calls, from cardiac arrests to hands caught in machinery to a naked person overdosed on drugs running around screaming. I had over 100 ALS contacts. I had worked hard as a young medic and was able to recover from my mistakes due to the pure call volume. I had passed. I wasn't able to drink at my graduation, but I had a license to administer morphine.

I worked briefly at AMR, my first job as a paramedic, and had a yearning to do something crazy. Where could I test and challenge myself in this field? Where could I go and explore the world? I applied and was hired for the Fire Department of New York. I also got my EMT boyfriend Kenny a job too, so we packed my Jeep Wrangler with practically everything I owned, and it was off to New York!

I had to go through an EMT academy for a few weeks and work as an EMT basic before I got reciprocity as a medic. The first unit I was stationed to was in Bellevue, mid-town Manhattan. I walked into the station with my EMT bag, and the first thing I got told to do was get someone in the office a cup of coffee. I was a newbie and no stranger of my humble beginnings. I came back with the coffee, and

Chapter 4

they asked me my status. I had stated I was a medic and working as an EMT to start off. Their demeanor changed completely. Just because I was a medic, I wouldn't do that to a new person, but thank goodness I wouldn't stay in Bellevue for long.

I got some interesting calls in Manhattan. I even got to work on New Year's Eve Times Square. Kenny was finishing up his shift and was back at the station; it was getting close to midnight for the millennium New Year's Eve event. I had a choice. Stay here and witness a once-in-a-lifetime opportunity of the clock striking midnight in Times Square or heading back to the station to be with Kenny. I chose the first one. Thankfully, things didn't work out for Kenny, and so ultimately, I made the right choice in experiencing this momentous event. There were so many units out that night we only got one drunk person and didn't transport. Lucky me. I even got to see and meet Mayor Gulliani when he was in office.

I then went to another upgrade academy to be a paramedic for New York City. I had passed my tests with the doctors. I was on my way to 03 X-ray in the north Bronx Jacobi station. I had two female partners, one named Sarah, who wore a million key chains on her belt a little crazy, and Dana, a down-to-earth medic who had a family. My memory of working with Sarah was when I had a patient en route to the hospital, and she stopped the ambulance or "bus," as you would call them, and opened the back of the door asking why I was starting an IV on the patient. I was new and, quite frankly, didn't have a real good reason. I would start IVs on everybody. Sarah saw that this patient was possibly a new-onset fib patient and left me alone. My crazy memory with Dana was that she was inviting Kenny and me over for dinner at the end of our shift, we got a 911 call, but I remember her driving to the local butcher before the call to get the meat for our dinner. I guess our priorities were a little different there. My other partners were just as crazy, hitting subway pillars with the bus mirror and flipping off other drivers while going lights and sirens. That's the way we rolled. I loved working with PD there. They were more present on our calls than the firefighters. I went to a shooting once, got out of the bus, and saw officers running past me with their guns drawn. The shooting was a robbery in the subway, so I would be heading downstairs to the station for what seemed to be safer.

We lived in a basement apartment in Old Mill Basin in Brooklyn, and it got tiring to be on opposite shifts with Kenny. Not a whole lot of time left to explore the city together, and I was turning twenty-one. I had concluded that I should either move above ground in a more uplifting environment or move home to be with my friends. I chose the second. My time in New York was over. I would visit there a couple of times later in the years. But I have a love-hate relationship with New York. The city, the people, the traffic, the difficult attitudes I would not miss. But the excitement, the food, the crazy calls I will put down in the books forever. I am glad I took a step of faith and worked for the famous FDNY.

It was back to San Diego, and I was employed by Rural Metro, a private agency that had the joint public contract with San Diego Fire. I worked there for a few years and got hired as a single role EMT/paramedic for San Diego Fire Department. My sister got hired before

Chapter 4

me, and I was so excited we were both working for such an amazing department. I had a goal of becoming a firefighter. I had many great stations I worked at. I did the first two years or so in San Ysidro medic 29 at the border under some pretty intimidating captains. I just hung my head low and did my probationary chores, washed the rig every day, and gained relationship with a lot of firefighter medics who rotated on the unit with me. I have my favorite partners, station, and crews, and one of them was Station 38 Medic 38 in Mira Mesa under Captain Rocco. He was like another father figure for me, and I really wanted to please him. We had a great station life; it felt surreal to be a part of a work family and really get along with everyone. I had finally gotten my chance after four-five years at the department, working hard, practicing interviews, and learning some of the ropes of what it would be like to be a firefighter. I had finally been accepted into the 64th Fire Academy.

Wow, the academy was something a little militaristic, but I loved the comradery I found with my brother and sisters in the academy. We had to wake up at the crack of dawn, go for a morning run, and be ready to hit the grinder the rest of the day, pulling hose, raising ladders, cutting roofs, crawling through tight spaces. All of it was overwhelming. Some stuff I excelled in, and in others, I was weak. I think the hardest part for me was the endurance of it all. I was more of a sprinter when I would run, and the timed three-mile run killed me. I always ran the hardest when I saw the finish line, and my academy captain could never understand it. The run would normally wipe me out. And then I had the remainder of the day to catch up. I was dehydrated, pulling hose in my turnouts all day, I wasn't eating enough, and I wanted so badly to be a San Diego firefighter.

It was a difficult day, and we were to certify on our hose pulls. I was struggling from the morning run and lack of water. I couldn't make the time pulling the hose up a three-story tower. Over and over, I tried, and finally, with some motivation from the academy captain, on my third try, I had made it. At the end of the day, he brought me to the front of the class and stated how strong I was to be the only one who was able to do a three and a half inches standing hose control first. My legs were strong as an ox. And he commanded it for me, saying I had what it took to compete in this academy, well as emotional as I was, I started to get teary-eyed, I'm not saying a full-on sob, but you could tell I was crying, yes I cried in front of my manly 64th fire academy, and I remember my friend just looking at me and giving me the expression to take a deep breath and hold it together. I think I did to the best of my ability, but I was really humbled at that point.

The academy got harder and harder for me. I had a green sheet which meant you were doing poorly, it was in truck operations, and if I got another green sheet, I was out. It was search and rescue day, and we had our facemask blacked out, and I had to do a search for a mannequin and a baby mannequin on the floor. I had a hard time dragging the heavy mannequin out of the building, so I learned a trick with my webbing to help drag them out. I found the adult and did just that. I then was looking for the baby. Now instead of going through a door and marking your door, I had entered from a window, you were supposed to find the male end of the hose, and that would

Chapter 4

lead you to the way out. With my air running out, I had the baby, and I couldn't find the male end of the hose to lead me out of the window. Now a part of me thought the instructor picked up the end of the hose and moved it. He didn't like me very much and was giving me a hard time. But honestly, whether it was the instructor who didn't think I was fit enough or God, it was God's purpose. I didn't find that hose line, and my air ran out, and I got my final green sheet. It was time for my dream of a firefighter to come to an end.

There was, however, a challenge I wanted to personally overcome. The three-mile run time in twenty-four minutes thirty seconds. I would run the timed run and come in last place; it was so hard for me, even the first place runner star would come to run with me on my last laps and support me. Even though I never completed the run time in the academy, afterward, I hired a running coach and was determined to complete this goal. I trained for months, doing long-timed runs. I took my running coach and boyfriend at the time to the academy site and ran my three-mile course. I got like 21:00. It was such an encouraging goal I reached, no one was there except for my coach and BJ, and I had completed a daunting task that used to weigh so heavily on my shoulders. I completed my three-mile run in 24:30.

After the academy, I went back to work for rural metro, it was hard to talk about it, but I was encouraged not to give up. El Cajon Fire Department was hiring a lateral paramedic, and I had my firefighter one from my previous reserve experience at Poway Fire Department. I had finally passed the lateral academy and went on to my field training. Now my FTO was a different experience and me being the only woman in the department has it own unique challenges. We had a major personality difference, and I ended up not passing probation. They had problems in the past with trainees passing, so I honestly knew I was an amazing paramedic. Did I verbally talk at the time about everything I wanted to do? No, but I was competent and able. I truly felt when I passed the lateral academy that I had a bad premonition with the department. It wasn't the exciting, thrilling accomplishment I thought it would be. But more of like a feeling of dread which was to come. I knew I just wasn't meant to be a firefighter. As I am writing this, my husband walks by and hears me sigh! Yes, that was a defeat in not becoming a dream of that of a firefighter.

It was back to the drawing board with Rural Metro, and it was after some years that I became sick with bipolar. I had taken three months off to recover and came back medicated and not knowing what to expect, quite frankly. I had been a medic for quite some time already, so it was like riding a bike. You never really forget it. I had gone through some medication adjustments, and I had an acute status patient. There was a young lady with hyperkalemia, which means they have high potassium in their blood. She showed some EKG changes. There was a specific protocol to follow when we had this type of patient. I wasn't too familiar, and these types of calls are rare. But we were to give calcium chloride and sodium bicarb to bring her blood levels back to a normal level. I heard my partner readout in our calcium chloride preload 100 mg; well, we were to give her 250 mg, so I thought I was to give her two-and-a-half preloads, which would be 250 mg, and I started to push it. Well, it was 100 mg per ml,

Chapter 4

so the 10 ml I just pushed was 1,000 mg. I stopped and realized what I was doing and called the base hospital to let them know. My patient started to throw up, and we got her safely to the hospital. The doctors and nurses were very sympathetic to my cause because a mistake is a mistake and everyone makes them. The normal dose for calcium was actually 1,000 mg, so I was not way off base. I had reported it, and my department medical director was concerned because I had previously reported all my mistakes like a good paramedic with integrity should, and they wanted to pull my license. I had met with the union and had been open and honest about what I was going through and my new diagnosis of becoming bipolar. I had gone through a medication change at the time and didn't feel quite myself. We informed them that I was covered under The Americans with Disabilities Act. After that, I worked with my medical director and personal psychiatrist to re-acclimate me to my position as a paramedic. I worked as an EMT basic for just about a year before returning to the field as a paramedic. They had me go through another field training orientation program, and I passed with a great preceptor. I will never forget the year of returning to basic training; it humbled me, it challenged me, it got me used to being on new medication while working with my sleep cycles. I had a Christian brother who was a new paramedic waiting to get promoted assigned to my basic unit. If it wasn't for him and his compassionate patient help, I don't know if I would have made it. I am thankful for those Christians who are the real deal out there.

I returned to the field and started to feel comfortable again. I had the worst call of my life, in difficulty and severity. My partner and I were driving to a motor vehicle accident, it was a minor injury, we were signing them against medical advice. And suddenly, I see these teenagers running down the side of the freeway yelling, "My buddy, help! Help! He is pinned." I took the ambulance up to the site of the crash, and I turned to my partner and told him to just pray. I wasn't sure what we were about to see, but I knew it would be bad. I got the gurney and equipment and made my way to the vehicle. I looked in the back seat, and the car was rear-ended, only when the impact hit the rear, it separated the rook of the car and caved into the patient's face. I told the patient to just slow his breathing down and relax that we were going to help him out. My partners on scene were telling me to call him dead it was so severe. My patient was still alive, responding, and had a pulse. We kind of just froze a little disconnected, and the firefighter on top of the car cutting and extricating the patient out told us to get a move on it, it reconnected us with the patient, and we began to remove him. Backtracking a month earlier, I had discovered on Youtube a call like this that was similar regarding the patient not having a structured face. I thought to myself as I briefly watched the video, and I hoped I would never have a call like this. Reflecting now, I feel like God was preparing me to see the worst. Once we removed the patient, he went into cardiac arrest, I went straight for a king airway which didn't need to visualize the vocal cords, and I placed it where I thought his airway would be. We ventilated and did CPR en route to the trauma center. I brought him to Sharp Hospital Trauma Center, and the surgeon commented that this was the worst injury he had ever seen. I placed

Chapter 4

him in the doctor's care and went outside to cry. I think this was the only time that I cried from a call, I had many distraught calls before, but this one, but this was a little different for me. They attempted to do traumatic stress debriefing, but all I wanted to do was talk to my partner and go back to the station. The next day I called to check on him, and I was told by the nurse that he survived, and his injuries were only facial. I was ecstatic. I was with my mother, and we decided to go visit him in the hospital. I walked into the ICU and unfortunately found out that he was indeed going to die; he was an organ donor, the cause was hypoxia. It was hard not to blame myself and think about what could have gone differently. The weird thing about the situation was his mother was there; her name was Rose, the nurse's middle name was Rose, and my last name was Rose. The patient ended up saving seven or so lives from being an organ donor. So, though his life was not spared, his life saved many others.

There are plenty of calls I remember strong emotional ties. Some days I can't even remember my first patient. But life moves on, and you just must learn and grow from your calls and do the best you can. I always go by the motto, "If you do your best, God will take care of the rest." He is the one who determines who lives or dies, and He calls the shots. I am just a mediator used to help what He determines fit.

I had felt the time was coming to commit to a new dream which I will write about later in this book, and that is to be a missionary in Thailand. When I got sick, I thought this dream was gone. I recall being in the living room of my house with my brother and sister-in-law Val and talking about how I could make this dream possible.

I needed to focus on what I could do, not on what I could not do. My ability, not disability. I took a leave of absence and fulfilled my lifelong dream to live and work in Thailand.

I had taken a three-month leave of absence and returned ready to work. I thought everything was going fine, I had previously sold my car, and when I returned needed to buy a bike to ride to the station and found a studio apartment close by until I got enough funds to buy a car again. I was functioning fine, but there was a call I went on, a simple diabetic emergency, and my hand began to shake. I was having tremors from the adrenalin I had. My hand was trembling as I was giving some simple medication. I had felt that it was time for me to lay down my career as a medic. I didn't want to jeopardize any patients and make sure I had a hold on this if I were to return.

I had really enjoyed teaching English in Thailand and thought I might take that route. I got a quick job with north coast church as a substitute preschool teacher, but that quickly faded, and I wanted to return to the medical field. I decided to work for the AMR Hemet division. I would work nights and weekends, went through yet another FTO orientation program. I never felt that I fit in with the people here. I did, however, have a strong EMT partner that was preparing to attend medical school. I had done something that got me fired. I had taught him how to do an IV on a patient. You technically had to be in school to do this, and though the same had been done for me when I was a student. You can't do this. I got caught by a supervisor, we didn't try to hide anything, and we were upfront with everything. They ended up fining me 2,000 dollars. I lost my job and decided to move to Orange County. I regret making that decision and decided from here on out to follow the rules with strict integrity. I think it came down to the fact that if God wanted me to do a different career, He would have directed me on a different path. But I truly feel I was called to be a paramedic. We all make mistakes or have sometimes shady things happen but how you recover, how you learn, and what you do from then on out determines your destiny. I was destined to keep on working.

I got a job in Orange County at Liberty Ambulance, which does a lot of ALS interfacility transports. This was paying a lot more, and my bosses didn't have a problem with my former trouble. I had paid my dues, served my time, and didn't want to waste the many years of experience I had. I got tired of doing interfacility; Liberty doesn't do any emergency calls. I decided to leave my field career and work for a functional medical clinic. They are an integrative medicine clinic that focused on natural medicine and IV therapy to treat various disorders. It was nice to have a nine-to-five job with weekends off.

The owners are amazing people, and I really like the way they treated us and ran the business. I cared for a lot of people who had Lime disease or autoimmune disorders. They wanted to focus on the root cause of a disorder rather than just treating the symptoms, and it created a healthy culture. I had some relational difficulties with my coworkers, but I learned a lot about how to manage emotions in the workplace, take accountability for my actions, and basically knew that I needed a different environment to grow at the time, so I decided to leave.

I went to work after that as a highly respected paramedic of twenty-one years to lynch ambulance. I was promoted to become one of the first-ever ventilator transport medics in Orange County, if not the state. I have been mentoring some EMTs in the right way, encouraging them, and leading them to do assessments. I feel like this was the right decision, and we just landed the Placentia 911 contract. I have talked with my doctor and feel that with my stability, it would benefit me to move forward in being a 911 medic again. I have done more emergency code three responses with this company and the skilled nursing facility patients we encounter than I have in the regular 911 system. Stroke codes, sepsis, hemorrhage, and major traumas, you have to be at the best of your game to make sure you give the best care to your patients. I truly enjoyed my time. It can be challenging to work full time, but if you care for yourself in regards to sleep, diet, exercise, and medication management, success can be yours professionally.

I had been running with my dog one day and ran into my best friend growing up, Jen. She runs a successful business called Peppy Lime, sharing essential oils and products with the community around her. I had dabbled into essential oils in the past when she first started but was careful to balance out medication and natural products. I will talk later about my journey. I joined her team briefly and shared my testimony with natural essential oils. My desire is to be healthy, balancing natural and modern medicine to treat my illness. At the same time, I got the inspiration to write this book. My hope is to encourage others with mental illness that they can work full time,

Chapter 4

they can accomplish dreams, they too can use this illness for their benefit and glorify God. You are not alone; you are capable, and your disability can become your ability to conquer amazing achievements in your life.

Chapter 5

"Then I heard the voice of the Lord saying, 'Whom shall I send? And who will go for us?' And I said, 'Here am I. Send me!'"

Isaiah 6:8 (NIV)

So I have a heartstring to Thailand. After my MMA career and the inspiration I received from Kru Mark as my master trainer, I felt even more connected. I had to find a way to go visit and serve. My first trip ever was developed by a friend I met from Impact. Her family was planning a trip to build houses on an island off of Koh Chang island. These islanders were unique because they had an adaptive pair of eyes to see underwater clearer; they could see things more effectively. We were to build houses on the shore. This was my chance, even though it wasn't what I expected. I was worried about so many things, like how would the time change affect my medication? Would I get sick again? What would happen if I'm on the island and in need of medical attention? I just had to rest in God, take a step out of the boat like Peter did and try to walk on water. It was then Peter sank when he took his eyes off Jesus and looked at his circumstances. I had to step out in faith and know that it was scary, but I felt it was God's will for me to go to Thailand.

It was a ten-day trip with a friend from Impact 195 and her family. We made the long plane ride to Bangkok and met our leaders, Mike and Judy. These folks were the real deal. They have been missionaries for Campus Crusade for Christ and had a boys and girls home they care for in Ranong. This was the town before we made the trip to Koh Chang. They ministered to the Moken village people who didn't speak Thai but their own indigenous language. We got into a small boat, I thought it would have been much bigger due to the fact that we had a two-hour trek on the ocean to the island. They had already gotten the lumber and wood on previous trips. When we arrived, it was so surreal and beautiful and a lot of hard work. We would begin to build the houses on stilts but had to mix the cement and then manually hold up the pillars while the tide was low. Then wait for the tide to get low again in the evening to finish the work. I would have to take my meds in the day and sleep and rest during the day since the time change was opposite. It was very difficult because I wanted to pull my weight off the work. I met some Thai Christians that would impact my life further down the road, Pi Sara and Pi Din. They became very good friends. We went around the villages and had Pi Sara translated in Thai and shared the good news of the gospel. Pi references someone being older in an honorable way in Thai.

As a little reward and break, we got a chance to go to the other side of the island and swim and take a break; it was beautiful. There were even some resorts. Kind of humbling: one side of the island is poor and humble, and the other side had a fancy resort. After our leisurely excursion, it was time to end the trip and head to Bangkok for some nightlife and markets and, to my surprise, I got to attend my first Muay Thai fight. I was so excited and thankful the team allowed

Chapter 5

for this to happen. My first trip to Thailand touched my heart so deeply, and I knew I wanted to come back again.

I had a fire in my belly about coming back and started to keep in contact with Sarah and Din. A local church was planning on going to Thailand and Cambodia to help a missionary out and serve in her orphanage. They were also planning a trip to India. I decided this would be a trip where I would go out and seek where the Lord would have me serve. I would plan to visit Bangkok, where my new friends were. We traveled to Chang Rai and Poipet, Cambodia, where the orphanages resided. I would teach a class on self-defense in Poipet to the street kids. I made my way to Chang Rai and stayed with Mike and Judy. It was a home away from home, and I always got the best advice from them. After the visit, I got on a bus to Chang Rai, and it was like the bus from the movie *Romancing the Stone*, which reminded me of the movie quote: "Is this the bus to Cartagena?" I got on excitedly to visit the next orphanage. Chang Rai was in more of an agriculture area, the kids were loving, and I taught a little there. Mama Marie was an amazing mentor as she has spent many years in Thailand. I still felt pulled to Bangkok, which is where I spent the rest of my time on the trip. I got an offer to serve at the orphanage but felt pulled to be with my friends from campus crusade at Shalom Church.

Bangkok bound, and I spent the time praying and had fellowship with friends from Shalom Church. My friend took me to one of my favorite places to fish. It was a manmade lagoon close by where we would catch giant catfish. They had a deck around the lake where they had hotel rooms. I always wanted to stay the night there, they also had waiters on bikes that you could order food from. Just an amazing place to fellowship and fish and hang out. There was also another outside manmade lake where they had other fishing. We would spend the entire day in the rain trying to catch. No luck there, but the view and the ambiance are something that I will never forget. It was time for me to go home and figure out how I would make the big move back to Bangkok.

I started to plan. I would sell my car, have a garage sale and sell my things and develop new ways to make money for Thailand. I cooked and had a Thai dinner party at my sister's house. Cooked pad Thai and my favorite dessert, Thai sticky rice with mango. It was amazing. I sold my car at a fair price and closed out my 401K because I quit my job as a paramedic. I had a decent amount to go to Thailand because it's quite cheap overseas. I even had a sell your Gold For Cash night fundraiser at my house. My mom and I were laughing the other day because my dad sold his gold tooth and donated the money. Who would have thought that would take place, lol. I was destined to be Bangkok-bound!

I was so excited to set sail, so to speak, for Bangkok, I had five suitcases, bought a new notebook, had a new projector, and was on a long flight. I am not the best flyer, but I always remember the scripture. The heavens declare the glory of God, and the skies proclaim the workmanship of His hands. This scripture has always brought me peace when I am flying. I landed in Thailand, and now it was time to find an apartment and find a job. There was an apartment complex across the street from the church, I hadn't even contacted them, but

Chapter 5

my friends stated they should have vacancy. There were some church members that lived there. I got a studio with a bathroom, microwave, and small kitchen, and no stove for about 250 a month. It had some air conditioning, and the cook downstairs had made me some dinners before. Her name was Cook Kai. I was always surprised how much traffic she had from the church visiting for her to cook, but no one invited her to church. On long hot days, I had a lime soda she made for me that was so refreshing. I had started to make friends with the food vendors I visited every day because I didn't have a kitchen. I only microwaved oatmeal in the mornings and some instant coffee before I made my way out in the town. I had needed to work there, and I didn't have a degree. So technically, I was illegal because I didn't have a work visa. I got hired because, quite frankly, I was a white, English-speaking American. I felt at peace for going against the grain because I was witnessing the gospel. I got a job at a middle school English teaching agency and taught a couple of different classes. This was fun. There wasn't a whole lot of expectation teaching, which was good for me because I generally do better independent and with not a whole lot of supervision. I would come up with different activities within the class. Whether it be a game or art activity, I even brought my projector to show a Jesus movie or The Chronicles of Narnia. Something fun for the kids.

I had an adult class; I always took the motorcycle taxis to class because they were cheaper. I always had to ask for a helmet because, most likely, people didn't wear one. We only got into one accident on the way to work. We politely said we were okay and agreed that there was no damage and continued with our day. My adult class was super fun. It was like a business that extended English classes for its employees. At first, I was trying to teach grammar and boring stuff. I had a student come up to me and suggest my protocol change. I ended up doing a lot more fun classes like English jeopardy and teaching them the gifts of the spirit or love languages. They really took to the games, and it was a lot of fun. I also taught at a Japanese kindergarten class with another English instructor. This was a little stricter but included reading English books to them. I even started to learn piano, and they had one! So, to my benefit, I played songs for them. It was so much fun and a great learning experience.

So, I had many classes and also some private lessons with a Chinese student. This was a one-on-one class. It was nice to develop a relationship with a student closer to my age. I would take the subway and motorcycle taxi to her once a week for an hour.

Thailand was a place for me to get lost. I loved traveling through the markets, getting bargains, trying new foods. My favorite food is gay yang which is BBQ chicken with sticky rice in a sweet sauce. This whole meal was probably $5. I also would get weekly foot and back massages for 5 dollars. This was so helpful in gaining relationship with the Thai community while working on my conversation. I loved playing piano, so I found an English-speaking Thai piano teacher at Yamaha music studio. I would walk the slums behind the church to the mall where the studio was and met a lot of locals along the way. I remember one day I saw the motorcycle taxis behind the church in the slums; they were watching Muay Thai, they invited me to stay

Chapter 5

and watch, and have a beer, seemed right up my alley, but I decided I would just continue on my route to the piano studio. There was a temple behind the church as well. I was told the monks were not allowed to talk with women, so when I walked by and one said hello, I would just yell out "God bless you" in Thai and run away. There were little kids back in the slums, fishing, and they had poor houses that you would walk through getting to the main street. Street kids would run up to you and play, and they were so happy. I would walk by this disabled man named Mut. I felt sad for him. He would sit in the walkway all day and just be friendly to those who would pass by. I decided to buy him some treats and sticky rice for like five-ten baht, super cheap, and began to see him every time I would go to piano lessons.

One day on my way to a lesson, I decided to bring him a bunch of treats and my laptop that would play the Jesus film in Thai. I wasn't sure if he would understand it or what his Muslim neighbors would say, but he seemed always happy to see me. When I finally decided to leave Thailand, I ended up donating all of my things I could not take on a plane to Mut and his family.

I also still had a desire to train Muay Thai in Bangkok. I lived by Ramkhamhaeng University, which had a local boxing gym. I would either jog or take a motorcycle taxi to the gym and pay a small price for a pro fighter San Choo Sei to train me with the pads. They always wanted me to do a boxing fight there, but I was at the point of my career I would rather lose in Muay Thai than win at boxing. I declined the opportunity. There were some interesting people that trained at the gym. I even met and trained with a member of a famous Thai rock band. I remember running to warm up at the track outside before we would hit our pads. Then on my way home, the streets were filled with vendors, outside music, and a busy environment. I truly loved every day in Thailand, experiencing the culture, whether it would be having dinner by myself, fishing, or a gym experience. I even joined a Thai language school to work on my conversation skills.

Even though my experiences were great, it was getting harder and harder with my friendships. I needed more English relationships. My best friend out there, Kanchana, was amazing, and she would shop with me, eat dinner, visit me in my apartment and listen to me talk about romantic feelings for Din. It was time I took a chance in sharing my emotions, or my time here was coming close to an end.

It was a rainy night, the men's discipleship house was down the street, and I decided to join the boys in indoor soccer. I was pretty good at playing my whole life, and I think they let me because I was an American. Thai women didn't typically play soccer. However, a lot of the church showed up to support. There were a lot of men from Africa who showed up to play at the complex; it was quite a happening spot. It released a lot of emotional energy, gained relationship, and was a great time.

It was time for me to share with Din how I felt about him. He was similar in age, and I was at the point where I would go home or move forward in relationship with dreams to make Thailand my forever home. I went to the male discipleship house and shared with him my feelings. He was surprised. I don't know if

Chapter 5

he understood the extent of them but only agreed to a friendship. Thai relationships are not like American ones in the fact that they literally take forever to develop. Friendships can go on years before they ever turn romantic, and my ideal was, let's get this show on the road. We ended up being friends.

I had to commit to being healthy there too and was a patient at Bumrungrad hospital, which had English doctors, and had to make sure I was getting a prescription of lithium as well. I believe the medication in Bangkok was a little different but sustained me enough.

I was ready to get home, I had been feeling lonely in Thailand, and my purpose had seemed a little unclear. I was making headway teaching and sharing the love of Jesus, but the relationships I was forming were slow and steady. I was extending my trip to the longest I could. I even went on an overnight crazy trip to the Laos embassy to get another ninety days in the country on a tourist visa. I had met amazing people, shared the love of Jesus, walked, shopped, and communicated with tons of locals and was realizing I was in a bit over my head. It was time to go home.

I had been feeling a little off coming home and had to go on some more medication for about a week. Luckily, God had not had me hospitalized again, and I can recover within a week with the right medication cocktail. I desire to get a tattoo that says, "pra yesu," which means "Jesus" in Thai on my wrist. I may have been there a short while, but the memories and the strength I gained there will last forever. I was truly a missionary in Thailand, there to share the good news of Christ in a Buddhist nation. I went through ups and downs, experiences, culture, and communication. Serving the poor and gaining relationship with the locals was one of the most amazing experiences I have ever had. Even if I took bold steps in reading scripture in the king's temple or giving up everything I had, gaining relationship with Mut, a disabled man, buying food from local vendors, foot massages to gain communication, and Muay Thai to gain strength. I loved every minute there and can't wait to bring my family back to share new and old experiences.

Chapter 6

*"Daughters of Jerusalem, I charge you:
Do not arouse or awaken love until it so desires."*

Song of Solomon 8:4 (NIV)

So things didn't work out exactly the way I expected with Din and Thailand. I had come home to regroup, reconnect, and move forward with my life. It had been a few years since Thailand. I took a break from paramedicine and was a preschool substitute teacher for a while, then worked as a caregiver where both my grandmothers used to live. I had a desire to get back in the field and worked at Hemet, which went terribly wrong, as I stated earlier. It was time for a change. I wasn't going to give up being a medic and decided to work in Orange County at Liberty ambulance doing interfacility transports. Not 911 anymore, but the pay was good. I had moved around a lot. I loved living in wine country, where my roommates were never home, and I could sit on my porch, have some wine, pray, and watch the distant thunderstorms. It was so surreal. But something was missing. I was missing my person, I had experienced so much in my life, and I wanted to experience the next chapter. To be a wife.

Now I may have gone about this in the wrong way; okay, I did go about this in the wrong way, but like the good old country song sang, "God blessed the broken road I was on." I had tried online dating, church singles group, just about everything on the list. Well, that is craigslist. I went on an online date once, and my suitor stated he answered a craigslist ad that to me was a bit scary; needless to say, our date didn't last long either. But I am open and honest and not about to play games with a man to get a decent free meal. Keep the drinks coming, though. It seemed like every date I would go on, we would hit it off online, then text and meet up. I had an interesting life, and I like to think I am an interesting person, so conversation flowed well for me. I would never think to disclose my health issues, and I clearly wasn't revealing any issues or bipolar swings. I don't think I ever have, only when I would get manic, which was one time and a couple of close calls. I was beginning to wonder if I would ever meet that special someone.

I was over dating men who were just in it for a booty call, who had girlfriends, or who were non-committal. I had always stated I am not looking for casual but something serious. I would like to get married and have children someday. I dated pilots, business executives, unemployed, construction, and drivers. I was open to finding my Mr. Right, and it didn't have to be a right job or car. You had to be Christian, although I did get to a point where I may have convinced myself to open that door too. I had already been involved with a non-Christian man for a year, and you know how that turned out. I have had successful relationships, two, so to speak, that were very healthy, exciting, fun, but both ended in heartbreak.

I thought I would take one last look, okay, so I probably would have kept up with online dating, but there was something different about this person. I was on a site called Zoosk. It paired me up with

Chapter 6

people who lived far away. I was living in Corona, this time traveling into Orange County. I saw this man was from Huntington Beach, his picture was great, somewhat of a rustic beard, looked like a mountain man, and if I can recall, one of the most intriguing things I read on his profile was that he was dedicated to his family. He was in the medical field, which in my book, is a plus. I decided to reach out. James was on the other end, over the online dating as well, and ended his membership. He saw that I liked his profile and decided to give this Zoosk another try. He signed back up just to talk to me.

I can remember the very first time we spoke. I was at work at a park, decided to take a walk, and we connected. We had a casual conversation, one that included his family life, children, and that he worked nights and was going to school at the time for cardiovascular technology. Busy man. I was a little more anxious to meet him, more so because I thought he was on the same page with me, but I didn't want to invest in yet another online date, taking weeks before you meet only to not have a connection. We decided to finally meet after talking on the phone a couple of times.

We agreed on one of my favorite foods: pho. It is not the best date food because I am usually making it so spicy that my sinuses are running, and slurping a big bowl of soup may not be so appealing as well. I pulled into the parking lot, and I wasn't sure what to expect. He greeted me as I walked up to the restaurant. He was friendly, attractive, and what could go wrong with having pho!

We sat down, and I had to teach him how to prepare the pho with the sauces and bean sprouts, ginger. Our conversation rolled smoothly as we talked about work and family. I remember how he would tilt his head, and he looked at me endearingly. It was time for the walk to the car, and I wasn't sure if we were going to have our first kiss. There were a lot of people around, and it wasn't very romantic or private for that matter. James had thought about kissing me too, but it was a little awkward. We gave each other a hug goodbye and looked forward to another date.

Things had been progressing quickly, and I was invited over to his apartment to watch hockey and have some beers. We may have also planned a walk on the boardwalk, but it was a rainy night. James took out his expensive craft beer he had been saving, and he went in for the kiss he missed the first date. I remember him saying he was looking forward to kissing me. I can't remember if he asked if it was okay, I think he did. We enjoyed a night of drinks and hockey, The Kings, his favorite team, and relaxed, something we still do to this day.

Our relationship was getting stronger and stronger, and it was time to meet a very special young lady in his life. Veronica. She was ten at the time and a fireball. I was coming up to his place to visit, and I remember as I was opening the door, she was just standing there dancing in the doorway. I had never had a serious relationship before with a man who had children, so I was a little intimidated; I really wanted her to like me. We played board games and watched TV and talked. It was an easy-flowing night. James had shared with me he had an older son and was previously married twice before. He had raised both of his children practically by himself, and both women were unfaithful. We had celebrated holidays together, and I met his son and father right before Christmas.

Things were progressing again, and I was trolling his Facebook, he liked a picture one of his marine buddies posted, and I got upset. James was going away to San Diego to visit his brother and wasn't giving me a lot of attention. I mean, I understand he was going on a vacation, but I was a little needy. We got into an argument, and he blocked me from Facebook. Yes, my future husband had blocked me. I think after a while, he reversed it. I was still shocked nonetheless.

I thought that we were over, and we hadn't talked in a week or so. I decided to talk with a gentleman from Alaska. I had always dreamed of living there and fishing and being a flight medic. Well, it turns out the Alaska man had a girlfriend. I remember confronting him about it, things were flowing so well, I couldn't believe it; it was over as quickly as it started, I was at work and was on the phone with Alaska, and James had beeped in. He told me how much he had missed me, kind of blew off our San Diego incident, and wanted to meet up. I remember this being a pivotal moment for me. I was always told you don't let your heart be your guide because, in the Bible, it says that your heart can be deceitful, so I lead my heart. James was a man of purpose, family, character. You don't come across that too often. I agreed to go and see him.

I went to his house like we planned to meet for another date since he worked nightshifts, he was sleeping, and I was left there knocking on his door for like half an hour. I was driving from Corona, so it was not a quick drive. I left, and halfway home, I got a call to ask for forgiveness for sleeping in hopes that I would turn around and meet. I knew this was another pivotal moment in that I said yes to James, no to Alaska, and confirmed that I was and had made the right decision.

We had been dating a few months, and we were sitting on his couch, and it was then that I told him I loved him. James didn't know what quite to say, he didn't really say much, actually. Things don't always play out storybook, but this was my story. I got upset, and he then opened to me that he was afraid and that he did love me. We talked about the seriousness of our relationship. James never thought he would be married again, but when you meet someone who has strong faith, character, and integrity, you don't let that person just slide by. I had shared with James the same night about my bipolar disorder, and it didn't even phase him; his mom actually is bipolar too, and he grew up with some interesting stories.

It was only a month later had we talked about the seriousness of our relationship, we were in it for the long hall. We talked about getting married. I think at this point, I turned into a crazy lady waiting in anticipation when he was going to propose. I had shared with him that I would like for him to ask my parents for my hand in marriage. And I even thought of my late grandmother's engagement ring, this ring is seventy or so years old, and I thought it would be perfect to hand down in tradition to be mine. James had asked my parents, received the ring, and now it was time for him to pop the question.

Like I said, I was going crazy, not literally just a girl who has been waiting years and years for this moment. I wasn't sure if it was going to be on the boardwalk at Matsu, our favorite sushi spot. He had planned

Chapter 6

a dinner reservation, and I was eagerly waiting to go anywhere that he was planning recently. We ended up going to the spaghetti factory. Now I am not going to lie and say I was not expecting something overly romantic or grandiose, but it's not the proposal that matters but the marriage. It reminded me of when my father proposed to my mother. He asked her to get him a cigarette out of the glove box, and in it was the engagement ring, not the most *suave*, but my parents did something right as they are over fifty years married now. James was afraid to do it on the beach for fear of dropping the ring, so he asked me over dinner, and my ring was amazing. I said yes and couldn't wait to get home to share with the world. I had finally met the one whom my soul loves.

We were excited and didn't want a long-drawn-out engagement. We had scheduled for our wedding to be in three months. Everything fell into place, family came and helped. I found the perfect wedding dress for an amazing price. We got married in Poway, California, at old Poway Park, which was an old railroad country-type setting. We got married in the gazebo, said our own written vows, and celebrated the night away. I was thirty-eight years old, had found the man of my dreams, it was a long wait, but God made it so clear and easy apart from some minor hiccups. What would our family look like? Would we have a family of our own? I mean, Veronica and James the 3rd are my stepchildren. I still have a desire to have a child of my own. I am just not sure if that is in God's will right now.

Moving forward, we decided on a honeymoon in Costa Rica six months later. It was amazing we decided to go to a resort my sister had been to before called Tabacon. It is in a rainforest. Our room was the honeymoon suite, amazing room with a huge swimming pool of a tub with a rain shower, and a view overlooking the volcano. Every afternoon there would be rainstorms, and we would just open the window, have a glass of wine, and relax in the ambiance. There were natural hot springs that filled the lagoons with waterfalls and, to our surprise, swim-up bars and private adult lounges. I remember one night we had an adult beverage during a thunderstorm and saw a huge iguana on a plant right by our spa. It was surreal.

We decided to go on an adventure, and that included zip-lining. However, I got freaked out. I am okay in America, where the safety standards are a little stricter. My husband, however, jumped at the idea. These lines were so high up. I waited at the end and made friends with some local horses. James said they saw some howler monkeys who started to throw poop at them. He ended up going on a huge Tarzan swing to top it off and ended it with a great experience.

I still wanted to do something adventurous. I mean, I was a former MMA fighter; thrill was the name of the game. Okay, well, after I got sick, life seemed to be a lot more precious to me, and I wasn't so gung ho anymore. I originally signed up for a white-water trip but heard some tourists talk about how it wasn't so safe. I decided to forgo that trip as well. We decided to take a rainforest walk over hanging bridges. Still high up, still thrilling, but a little more my pace. We met our guide, paid him twenty bucks, and he took us for a guided trail walk through this amazing rainforest, and yes, it was raining a little as we walked through, which was even more magical. We saw all kinds of different birds, and I was on the lookout for a sloth. They are nocturnal, so they

Chapter 6

are a little bit harder to spot. At the end of the trail, to my surprise, we spotted one, he was high in the trees and even moved his face a little, so we could see it through the binoculars. Truly a divine experience worth doing or experiencing again in Costa Rica.

So, on goes the honeymoon, and we are living in Huntington Beach, an excellent neighborhood with down-to-earth people, our favorite brewery Four Sons, and local restaurants we have come to love and appreciate. Dog parks, Central Park, Huntington Pier, James's dad's house are all close by and comfortable. I loved our apartment complex, though it had the occasional homeless person digging threw the trash, our neighbors were great, I felt like we always had second celebrations after the holidays, we would get together in the courtyard, have a drink, even if it was over a BBQ grill fire pit. Much better than the expensive fire pit we have currently in our backyard, minus the amazing people.

We decided to look for a place to buy because my husband is a veteran, a former Marine oo rah semper fi; he is currently mad at me for thinking it was hoorah, not oorah. He takes his Marine Corps with pride, as he should. I am so proud of the leadership the corps have taught him, and I know we understand the relationship called brotherhood. He gets a veteran loan for his service, which helps us out a lot. No money down and after a long, long process of yes at times yelling at our broker. We had no closing costs. I am currently blessed with our new condo, first-ever homebuyers. Upgraded wood floors, fireplace, A/C, and a bar. Oh, and a nice place for laundry! That I am truly excited about not having to slip my clothes to the downstairs laundromat once a week. We also have our puppy pit bull Nova that fits in nicely too, with an extra big backyard for a condo.

Our relationship has its struggles. I think with my bipolar I can go through times of just wanting to work less; sleep is a major important factor for me, and I worry about what it would be like to have a baby, endless nights, baby crying, not a whole lot of time to myself. I've been accustomed to having some downtime with coffee and sermons in the mornings, long walks with my dog. I don't know what I would quite expect because I have only had experiences through my family having children. Sometimes my husband worries about work and money the most. I currently work full-time as a paramedic, and I get tired. It's hard because I think I need more rest, and my husband is an amazing provider, always worried about money and working. He has provided for this family tremendously, he works as an echo sonographer for the VA Long Beach. It is his dream job, a vet serving vets, his passion for family and country and fellow service people illuminates off his work ethic and character. I love hearing stories of him praying for his patients and how God uses him to touch the lives of others. My husband has just been awarded a great percentage for being a disabled vet. He served in Desert Storm as an amphibious assault team leader and has struggles of his own with PTSD. We are in a marriage with both parties struggling with mental health problems, and if it wasn't for our strong faith, church community, and family, we probably would be another statistic. We try to make the best decision possible but sometimes get put in difficult circumstances. One step at a time, and if it's one thing I learned, is sometimes when

Chapter 6

you step into what God has called you to, there will be opposition. "New level, new devil" is what Joyce Meyers always says. Sometimes when you experience all God has for you, there can be challenges in your professional life and your marriage. I believe when you are amidst your breakthrough, weird things start to happen. Especially when you are writing a book, so press forward, keep on keeping on. There is not one person who has succeeded who hasn't gone through rejection and failure. I just want to make sure I am on the right path, but as Joyce says, if you get lost, don't worry, God will find you. I like the fact that I am moving forward. It's like driving a car, you move forward, and at the right time, God will direct you to turn right or left, but you will get nowhere if you are not driving and staying idle.

Our marriage has its ups and downs, but for the most part, we are good, yes, I want more time off from work to rest, but I just need to be more purposeful with my time. To think about adding a child to the mix is quite intense. We did, however, recently decide to adopt another pit bull/shepherd puppy; I don't know if we are in over our heads on this, but our current pit bull Nova is super needy, and loving it would be great for her to have a little sister. We named her Scout. I always wanted a dog named Scout, and here she is. James let me name her. We get her next week after she has been microchipped and spayed. I didn't do well with Nova being spayed, she got sick after the surgery, and we had to take her in to get Sub Q hydrated. It was horrible letting her go the morning of. I was crying and praying over my little puppy, I couldn't even imagine what it would be like for a real baby. Nova is our fur baby, but you know what I mean.

We have been trying for a real baby for over a year or so. I was on lithium which can be known for having some potential birth defects. It was time that I transferred over to a healthier drug. We found a psychiatrist who specializes in fertility with bipolar, as well as making an appointment with a high-risk pregnancy doctor. I struggled with questions to myself, such as should we even have kids? Would it be safe? What if they turned out with a mental illness? What if it brought me back into a manic state? Changing medications is not something I ever look forward to; you get stable with consistency, you get on a protocol that is regular and predictable. The doctor wanted me to switch to Latuda, which is better for the baby. I was on a mission now to get off lithium, which I had been on for over five years. A lot of scary going on, but I was ready to move forward in faith.

We would taper off the lithium and increase the Latuda. Now, this medication isn't cheap, it was costing us at first like $250 a month until we got on a special savings plan. I was feeling okay other than some increased anxiety, she gave me a prescription that was pregnancy safe that helped anxiety; it was an antihistamine. I only had to take it once while at work, and it was just fine, it didn't cause me drowsy and alleviated my symptoms. It's been month after month of trying, and still no luck. I was hoping not to get pregnant over my trip to Spain and France in the summer well because you know I wanted to eat, drink and be merry and not worry about that while on vacation. It didn't happen, and it still hasn't happened. I think we might call it quits in a couple of months and realize maybe it's just not in God's will for us. The reason we wanted another child is that I

Chapter 6

really had an amazing childhood. So many great memories of playing with my brothers and sisters, great holidays, and the love our family had to give. I love being a stepmom to my twelve-year-old daughter. I have to say we don't quite have that mother-daughter bond as if I were to raise her as a baby, but we do have a connection. I see how Veronica and her dad have a bond, always snuggling and saying, "I love you," I wish I was there, but the truth is I am not. I know it will take years to formulate a tight connection, and I just pray that God forbid anything were to happen to James, me, and Veronica would go on to have a loving relationship. I would be there for her wedding, and she would visit me in a nursing home when I am old and gray. James also has an amazing son who is twenty-five years old. I hope that I can gain a better relationship with him as well. One thing that my family keeps telling me is just because they are your blood relative doesn't mean they will be there for you. I have a loving family, nephews mostly, and I have peace now. If I don't have a child, I will have a fulfilling life, and it wouldn't define me.

Chapter 7

"Jesus turned and saw her. 'Take heart, daughter,' he said, 'your faith has healed you.' And the woman was healed at that moment."

Matthew 9:22 (NIV)

Would I be healed, or wouldn't I? I knew no matter what happens in life, the daily grind, I would try to continue to have a positive attitude. God was healing me day by day though countless medication trials, diet change, exercise, and natural remedies. I believe it all helped and was all in good balance.

When I first was put on medication, it was called Geodon. Now this one was hardcore, I had ocular issues in the hospital where my eyes would cross each other; how scary when no one was telling me what was going on. My mother and I were having a conversation the other day about what it was like with me being in the mental hospital. She had relationship with the doctors at Sharp Mesa Vista because she was a psych nurse previously there. She said one day she called to see how I was doing, and the doctor said I was spread out flat on the ground like a crucifix and not moving by the elevator. I do remember that briefly in the fact that I was surrendering my whole self to the Lord, to beg Him for mercy and healing to be completely humbled. Looking back, yeah, I was sick and in need of medication. I am glad they had a somewhat good sense of humor about it, and we can look back and chuckle a little. Proverbs 14:13:

"Even in laughter, the heart may ache, and rejoicing may end in grief." I feel this scripture holds a lot of truth. There was a lot to look back at and share a laugh in the grief that I shared. You do some silly things when you are manic, and I am glad my family can share in that laughter with me as though it were good medicine. Anyone else and I would probably punch in the face.

The Geodon put me back a lot. We started on a small dose when I was originally sick, then when I was diagnosed bipolar, we went with a full dosage and lithium. It gave me somewhat of a somber look on my face. I would be feeling fine, and I constantly would have people asking me if I was okay or upset about something sometimes, I still get asked this question. I could be perfectly at peace inside but live my outward expression was solemn. I believe they called this solemness. I remember my friend in Impact 195 turned out to be bipolar also. I didn't quite go into this earlier, but I believe it was destined to be that God would have placed those with mental illness around me to comfort and support me.

I seemed to be writing during my up phases or my hypomanic phase, and then I take a dump, want to sleep a lot, and do not seem to get any writing in. I have been through a period in my life where I had to find the right medication to work, the most stable one I would be on would be lithium. You must get your blood levels checked every so often to make sure you don't get into toxicity. I had been working out at the MMA gym, and I think the sweat levels would throw me off balance. I felt kind of dizzy and off. But lithium is not good for babies because it can cause heart defects. I also tried other medications like

Chapter 7

Zyprexa, which pretty much blew me up weight-wise. It is known for that, and managing my weight has been a struggle otherwise. But the Zyprexa really helps stop any craziness from happening as far as manic episodes are concerned. It would usually take me about a week to recover, but it was kind of like having a bad cold and needing to sleep all the time. It hits you like a truck, but it does the trick, I only had to do that one time before I went to Thailand. I would try to stay off an antipsychotic and just use lithium, but I think I needed something, sometimes a little more balanced.

Now that I was at the end of my childbearing years, it was time to do something major. I had to finally come off lithium and adjust to a neutral baby-making medication called Latuda. I was nervous about this, but I had a stable job, good hours, low stress for the most part, and it was time to wean myself off lithium. This surprisingly went well, I think I just had some anxiety or panic issues where I would take an antihistamine, and that did the trick, it didn't make me drowsy or anything. The Latuda was expensive at first, around 250 dollars a month, but finally, through the insurances we had it got covered, and there was a patient discount card that helped. It's unfortunate that some people can't afford the right medication that would be best for them. I have been on Latuda for a couple of years now, and sadly still no baby. I just turned forty-one, and now I am wondering if that part of my life will come to fruition. A lot of my friends have older children, and they are phasing out of that moment in time for them that I haven't even experienced. Yes, being the world's greatest aunt has some amazing benefits, and being a stepmom is fabulous too. But I still wonder what it would be like to have my own. We just got another puppy, a sister for Nova, my pit bull, who is actually my emotional support animal. We got a doctor to register her, so we didn't have to pay a pet deposit at our old apartment complex. And they didn't allow the type of breed. She is the sweetest ever and cuddles with me all day, even lets me sleep in, that is until we got Scout. If it's one thing I like to depend on, it's sleeping in, but getting up early and getting over the morning grouches has helped me focus on some other things and having more quiet time for the Lord in the morning. It balances me to get up, get Veronica to school, clean the kitchen, diffuse some oils and get ready to tackle the day.

On to my adventure with essential oils, I had dabbled with them many years ago, and it wasn't the right time to wean off my sleep medication. I had tried to use them more than my meds. And I was coming close to another episode. I remember I was using copious amounts of frankincense to bring more clarity and focus, which helped, but I think I was overdosing on oils. Yes, you can use too much. I reconnected with one of my best friends growing up, and she is an amazing advocate and representative for essential oils. I introduced them back into my daily regimen. They are phenomenal, and let me just give you a brief lesson on how oils are effective. When you smell oil, the oil travels in your nose, obviously into your olfactory bulb, which is in your limbic system. The limbic system is the emotional powerhouse. It controls emotional memories. When you take a smell like pumpkin pie, for instance, it can trigger a strong memory and emotion of the last time you smelled that scent.

Chapter 7

Reminding me of coming home from school to my mother baking, or having Thanksgiving dinner, a homely comforting aroma that stirs up feelings of relaxation, joy, and a warm sense of wellness. The hippocampus controls memory, and your amygdala controls fear, anxiety, anger. Having a calming scent or one that brings memories of calmness can directly affect your emotional powerhouse of the brain and change the way you feel, act and behave. The essential oil particles are one in that they can penetrate the blood-brain barrier in the brain where certain medications cannot. The blood-brain barrier is selectively permeable, which means, what is stated earlier, some substances can cross it while others cannot. Essential oils can pass the barrier.

In the morning, I like to spray citrus fresh, which kind of wakens my senses; it's uplifting and invigorating, giving me an energized state. Then its valor and stress away blend. Valor can help be a mood enhancer and stimulate feelings of courage and confidence, a blend I like to stick with while preparing for my paramedic job. The stress away is just that it balances out the emotions of stress and brings an uplifting scent to the mix. My go-to for relaxing, which I can't seem to live without, is peace and calming blend. I love to diffuse these oils because of the direct entrance into my limbic system through the olfactory bulb. Peace and calming are pretty much what it says, it comforts me and relaxes me, it goes well with hallmark on and a glass of wine with my husband. Something I cherish. Some other scents I like to diffuse in the morning are thieves, I feel better with a clean kitchen, and this immunity, bacterial buster does the trick, the smell of cinnamon also brings a scent of comfort. I am also experimenting with peppermint and citrus fresh blend to wake up my senses and motivate me during the afternoon slump; this and a cool cup of ice coffee seem to do the trick. And lastly, frankincense and lavender, which I call frankly focused, bring the calming scent of lavender and the spiritually focus-minded frankincense, I like to diffuse this when I need to be spiritually uplifted and meditate.

Oils have been quite a delight for me. I hope to share them with the elderly community and family and friends. I have gotten to love the tight net community of natural healing. Even though I use them as a complement to my medication regime, and as a disclosure, you should not go off your medication and do oils in place. It seems to pair quite nicely but not solo. Anything and everything I can do to bring balance is a must. I just wish I could do that with the exercise in my life. I love to walk my dogs every morning around the lake or to the park, but I think the years of overworking out kind of sucked the life out of me. That is another avenue I wish to tackle. I am not happy being this big, but I am comfortable, I think I would rather have a few pounds on me, enjoying a good wine or beer and some amazing food than worry about what I look like. My husband sees me as beautiful, and that's what matters the most. I do want to be at a healthy level, though, and make sure my heart is good. I am just not the way I used to be, and I am okay with that; balance is key.

I have recently received more inspiration from Veronica as she has joined the wrestling team. Fast forward a few years after writing this chapter, she is fifteen now! And I will dive a little deeper later

Chapter 7

about what that's like, but as a former pro fighter, I am super proud of her competing. It has encouraged me to take my physical health a little more seriously. I recall working out for five hours a day, pushing it to the limit, running every day. I have tried several Muay Thai gyms, and I just can't seem to find what I am looking for, either I have a disconnect with the coach, or the workout regiment is what I am used to. I have tried everything from beach body online home workouts to getting an expensive peloton. I am certain my weight will continue to be a struggle being on psych meds. Veronica has wanted to increase her stamina and strength for her wrestling, so I am looking into some simple kickboxing workouts that include strength and conditioning. Small steps lead to big steps. My focus is on family time and not gym time, so like I said, balance is the key!

Veronica was getting ready for her first meet and had been a bit anxious, I have told her it's okay to cry, just not in front of everyone. I am a passionate fighter, and I have had an emotional time or two in the ring. But kept it privately. I was on my way to meet her and just quietly prayed that I wouldn't miss her match, one thing led to another, and I finally found her at the starting line, she was jumping up and down, stretching, and looked confident before the fight! I got teary-eyed watching her get ready; she fought hard, was technically sound, got a couple of reversals, and came so close to winning. It was, for me, the best stepmom moment to date, and I can't wait until she experiences what it's like to fight and train hard and get that hand raised for her first win. This is what motivates me to put down the wine glass, get up and take my exercise more seriously. I might not be where I was before, but I can take my health to the next level to help lead my stepdaughter on the right path to becoming a champion.

Chapter 8

"As they sailed, he fell asleep. A squall came down on the lake, so that the boat was being swamped, and they were in great danger."

Luke 8:23 (NIV)

So, a year has gone by, and we have been planning our fertility journey, month after month of nothing happening, disappointment after disappointment. We finally put the thought in our heads to try IUI, intrauterine insemination. Basically, take fertility meds and have James's little swimmers meet my egg by watching closely and a trigger shot to release the egg. It is expensive, but we have Kaiser insurance, so it covers some of the costs. We cannot afford IVF as much as I would like to. So we finally saved up the money, began testing, and got our blood work done. The HSG test was one they check to make sure your fallopian tubes are working; well, this was a horrible test for me, and the first radiology department I went to could not get the catheter inserted, stating I had possible cervical stenosis. This got my head spinning, and I decided to reach out to my OBGYN to have it evaluated, she said it was fine, but my second HSG test was costing me a lot of money, and the second doctor had an initial hard time. But finally, was able to perform the test. All I remember was praying everything was fine, and it was. So we had our phone consult with fertility doctor; my AMH was super low, 0.18, which needs to be over 2.0. This means that my ovarian reserve is super low, and I don't have many eggs left. Tough decisions and a little bit of discouragement. I have been listening to my annual song that makes me think of having a baby, which is Josh Groban's "Believe" from *The Polar Express*. I remember I was in the genetics department ten years or so earlier watching this movie in the waiting room when this song started playing. It gives me hope and fans the flame in my heart to have a child of my own. Now I decided to add Disney songs to power it up. I love baking with my stepdaughter Veronica and listening to my Disney playlist; this would include songs from *Moana, Tangled, Princess and the Frog, Frozen,* and *Toy Story*. Gets me in a positive, hopeful mood.

It had been day after day of injections, not drinking wine which I love to do; I even have my WSET level 2 certification, in which I took an extensive class under a master sommelier to get, so I have been sacrificing and remaining hopeful. It was finally time for IUI day. I had my husband's lucky eagle socks on and, after the procedure, listened to my two favorite songs to give me hope. The two-week wait was hard, but I finally got my period and found out that our dreams of becoming pregnant were probably not going to happen. I have some that still say I am young, but I am trying to change my focus to things that I would enjoy with older kids, traveling more, sleeping in, date nights with the hubby, and weekend getaways. Maybe this new normal for me would be okay. I am still a little sad that I most likely won't have a biological child, but that doesn't mean I can't pour into my stepchildren.

We had gotten a new dog a year earlier. As I told you already, her name was Scout, a name I had always wanted to name my dog.

Chapter 8

We finally had her, and it had been a tough year, lots of chewing, barking, and difficulties, she had finally started to mellow out. When we decided to have her trained, we noticed that she had a dented skull, her facial muscles started to atrophy, and we took her to the vet. We soon found out we needed to see a neurologist, that appointment didn't go very well either, and she needed an expensive MRI test done. We contacted the rescue we got her from and did a fundraiser, the whole test came to around 3,800. We finally raised all the funds, half with the rescue and most with our own personal loans. Our precious Scout had a brain nerve stem tumor and was expected to only live for six months to a year. We were devastated. I have dealt with life and death for over twenty years in my profession, but this really hurt us emotionally as a family. We would focus on giving her the best life. Lots of yummy dinners of green beans and pumpkin, walks with Nova, and endless cuddles. She began to become more and more off balance. These past three months, October through December 2020, seem to be a season of struggle, sadness, and disappointment. It was December 15 at 1:30 p.m. we had our sweet Scout go to be with the Lord. We had a home vet come in and do the end-of-life procedure. We wanted Scout comfortable with her loved ones, on the couch, and eating some of her favorite foods. I prayed to God to give me a sign that she would be okay, that she was in heaven on green pastures, playing with our past loved ones. I had played Josh Groban's Christmas playlist from the beginning, and when she was given the injections, it was on the song "Ave Maria," when she entered heaven, it was angels we heard on high. She had a big cheeseburger that she loved and devoured, she rested on James's lap, and the next moment she was with Jesus. I really struggled after her death to just connect with her; the few days after, I could feel warm spots and the end of the bed where she would lie and almost sense her presence. We got her urn and a paw print a few weeks later as she was finally home. Our family had a handmade portrait of her done for Christmas that brought tears to our eyes. People who aren't pet lovers or have dogs of their own don't really know how close they can be, they are members of your family. With my infertility especially, my pups feel like my children. I still make my bed nice and cozy for her spirit to lay on. I just can't help but sense a big celebration or special person that has passed that God wanted to share Scout with my husband is a marine, and he always says she will be there for him to guard to heavenly pearly gates when he goes to meet Jesus one day.

The death of Scout and some recent deaths at work really have me facing some trying times. I realized after a particularly gruesome call at work that I needed some much-needed therapy. PTSD in our family runs deep with James being a marine serving across seas during a time of war and me as a paramedic for so many years. I can have flashbacks, stress, tension, nightmares. I had a double homicide at work where two young twin girls were stabbed to death in their sleep by their father, who later committed suicide. This is a particular club you don't really want to be associated with at work. The calls that make you cry, the ones that keep you up at night and fearful to show up at work the next day to see what next call you get. I want to participate in EMDR therapy, which helps you emotionally process the disruptive calls I've been on. I have, at this point, been wanting to leave my calling as a paramedic, but the Lord just seems to not release me yet. My priority is my family first, my health, and next would be helping people. I know I am an exceptionally experienced good medic, and I have come to a crossroads of where my professional career will take me. Countless hours watching sermons, praying, and journaling, I need to see and be obedient as to where God is leading me. I am committed to the EMDR process to see if I can make my work life less stressful and fulfill God's purpose for me there. I have also been deeply motivated to start my writing and speaking to help those who have mental health challenges. Like writing this book, but that would entail me coming out to the world with my secret. What would my coworkers think? Family and friends that don't know? I have to be at the point in my life where my message is clear, and I have surpassed some of the major challenges my life has presented.

2020 has been a doozy. we have had the COVID-19 pandemic, political crisis, fertility failure, death of Scout, and life and death situations to process at work. I realize that we will go through lots of different seasons and changes. Grief and loneliness. It reminds me of the quote, "Change is inevitable, and it's one thing that we resist the most." I also lost my original partner at work, and two days after the new year, we were up at the cabin in Big Bear, and James had slipped on some tile from trailing the wet snow that was outside. He has torn his meniscus and will need surgery at the end of the month. I would be lying to you if I were to say that I am doing okay with it. My PTSD and thought of death are creeping in there. I just cling to Jesus, and His quiet presence is telling me everything will be okay.

This has forced us to take a good look at our health, our life decisions, and make some changes for the coming new year. We have tried Keto, beach body, and many different diets, so we are taking a break from cooking and attempting Nutrisystem for a little bit. We were also blessed with a peloton that is coming in a couple of months due to backorder, and walking Nova around the lake has brought on some much-needed prayer time. I guess the new year is a perfect time to reflect, renew and replace old habits into a fresh new start. I think the thing I look forward to the most is I know the season of struggle and strife must end and a season of blessing, growth, and newness is to come. The trick of this all is to have joy during the pain. There are many moments I will cherish during these past three months. October was my birthday month, carving pumpkins and visiting our favorite winery, the fresh fall leaves and autumn season. Watching scary movies with popcorn with the family and making pumpkin bread. November is Thanksgiving, and getting together with family despite Covid, new recipes, and a cooling of the air, hikes in Big Bear at the cabin. December getting our favorite Christmas tree, special nights by the fire with Scout and Nova at our side, watching Christmas movies with our favorite bottle of wine. There are moments of joy and warmth to be had during the storm, to not take life for granted, and to keep on keeping on.

Chapter 8

Fast forward a year later to now 2021, and I think the holidays always have me wanting to nest, so to speak, and my desire for continuing our family progresses. We came into some blessings financially, and again even after my IUI experience, ideas of growing our family kept coming up. We would investigate IVF after long consideration and facing the fact that even with treatments our percentage to have a child is 15 percent, and I can't even stress how much IVF is, as I am sure everyone knows. I was faced to either publishing this book and focusing on speaking engagements or taking that journey down the with IVF. I chose what you are reading now. Of course, I would like to have everything, but we wanted to be wise with our money and kind of face the fact that it didn't seem like having more children biologically was an option. We are considering adoption or foster care but later. I have come to embrace that my and James's lifestyle will conclude more with our mission to serve others with better mental health, travel, and discover new food, wine, and cultures. Something we both love to do. We will focus on Veronica finishing high school and, of course, encouraging her in her advanced studies, but I don't know if living in California will be in our later future.

Chapter 9

"Whether you turn to the right or to the left, your ears will hear a voice behind you, saying, 'This is the way; walk in it.'"

Isaiah 30:21 (NIV)

Decisions, decisions, decisions. It's the new year, and despite the first few days being at urgent care with my husband, I have been reflecting a lot on what path to choose. How do you know what's God's plan and will for your life? Will people think I am crazy when I say that I sense God directing me a certain way? Well, I do have a little bit of crazy in me, but one thing I know for sure, when you sense God speaking into your life, step out and find out to see if it is actually Him. God doesn't want to lead you astray, and as long as you are in the word, listening to wise counsel and taking steps of faith, He will direct your path, and if you have chosen wrongly, don't worry: He will let you know and begin to guide your path.

I have reflected lately on my decision-making abilities and have recently studied on my personality traits. See, I am an ENFP, for those of you who don't know what that is, it's a personality put out by Meyers Briggs. I find this extremely helpful in reflecting why I am the way that I am, deepening who God made me to be, and how my mental illness speaks through my personality, what my personality is, and figuring out how my bipolar affects it. I am a campaigner, someone who can motivate, inspire, lead and fight for justice. I am a jack of all trades and can have many different interests. The E is extrovert, N intuitive, F for feelings, and P for perspective. I have the innate ability to read a room, my intuition has mostly never led me astray. It has helped me in becoming a good communicator and resolving conflict. The downside to my personality is that when I am stressed out, I can be very critical and negative. Which usually happens when I am having someone try and control me. I don't do well with a micromanager. It's interesting that I have been a paramedic after all these years in a hierarchy type of structure, but what I excel at most is managing the chaos that comes with it. They have said that one of the best qualities for a campaigner would be to drop them in a situation of crisis and chaos and watch them manage and solve the problems. Lately, I have been reflecting and contemplating my leadership. I have a potential promotion opportunity at work, and I have been going back and forth on whether to go for it. I had decided that my indecision is a decision, and I want to at least interview for it. If I am not chosen for the position that is out of my hands, but in preparation for this, I have done a lot of self-realization and growth. I am not a procedure type of person or like to follow an organized list. I am not savvy with electronics and find training manuals a bit boring. But what I do find strengthening is my ability to empower others, solve problems, and help people. To read a room, to communicate a problem out with my superiors, and to have an influence with my years of experience. I know that I am a leader, but I must be passionate and motivated and really care for the purpose. It hasn't been decided yet, but I am starting to really dig deep with how I make decisions.

Chapter 9

I have recently studied and read a book by Andy Stanley called *Better Decision, Fewer Regrets*. It talks about the five questions to have when asking yourself when approached with an important decision. I have been very reactive in the past emotionally and would like to be more responsive. Taking a step back and detaching myself from the emotional side of a choice and asking myself what would be the wise thing for me to do? What is God's will for my life? The first question was, am I really telling myself the truth? The truth is I don't like such a stressful job, but God sometimes asks you to do things you don't particularly want to do, I know it's a calling, and I am waiting to see when I am released from it by Him until then I will walk forward in faith, face my fears, and be obedient to the places and tasks He has put me in. The second question is what kind of story do you want to write? Your life is a story, and I want my life to be a legacy. I don't want to quit, and I want my story of perseverance to spread to the world, that even though you may have a setback, like bipolar is for me, a medical diagnosis, that you can achieve amazing things for God. He has a purpose for your life, and if you have faith, take risks, and pursue your dreams because they can come true. I decided that I want to write my book and share my story not only to help others who have struggled with mental illness but to document my story for my family and future grandchildren. I may not ever have a biological child, but I will have my stepchildren and nephews to influence. I want to leave paramedicine with dignity and grace, fulfilled in helping all that I could, empowering new medics to make wise decisions, and in God's timing. The third question is, are you paying attention to the tension? When faced with a decision? A person to date, a job to take, somewhere to move. Is there a red flag? Is there something in your conscience that's alarming you to do otherwise? I can guarantee that my professional fight career would have gone a different direction if I hadn't dated the people in my team. There were many alarms going off in my heart in my head and with the wise counsel around me. When you sense a tension or a red flag, pause and wait to make the decision, explore and pray for God to reveal to you the next moves, and I can't stress it enough. Have the faith to be obedient to what He wants for you. Question number four, what is the wise thing to do? Sometimes we just need to ask ourselves what that exactly is. Responding and not reacting, I have been focusing lately with my leadership opportunities. What would a great leader do? With my past experiences and my future opportunities, what would be the wise thing to do? God's Word states when you ask for wisdom, you will receive it. Getting wise counsel is also important in your life, following positive examples of leadership in your life. The last question is, is this a loving thing to do? Relationships are key and if what you are doing is not loving maybe there is a different approach. This has helped me use my intuition skills to read people and their motives and make a loving decision despite how they may be treating me at the time.

    I remember a story that my pastor once said, a plane can change the course of its destination, little by little; the tiniest change can effectively turn you off course and land you in a completely different destination. It's important to make decisions wisely and learn from

Chapter 9

your past mistakes. Following guidance from the Holy Spirit will never lead you wrong, journaling your thought, reading God's word, having wise counsel, and taking those obedient steps of faith will lead you to God's will for your life.

So with all these decisions circling me, I decided to pull out of EMS for a while. I had returned to a previous job I had at a functional medicine clinic. Here we treat the root cause of the illness. Enhancing diet, exercise, supplements. It can sometimes be very routine, but I have these simple conversations with patients that are suffering from their illness, and it is a chance to bring some hope to them. I am at the finishing end of my probation, and I am encountered with another decision. I set an appointment up with the owner and doctor of the clinic, and I will be potentially telling them my underlying medical issues. I don't know yet if I will go through with it, but I would like to try some treatment modalities for my bipolar. I just would like more energy to be able to live my life more fully again. When I am hypomanic, I feel great, exercise a lot, my personality is illuminating, the world is my oyster! I am interested in trying NAD, which stands for nicotinamide adenine dinucleotide. It was originally used for alcoholics and drug addiction to suppress the desire to consume, but it has so many additional benefits which are helping you on a cellular level, it creates energy, helps produce neurotransmitters, aids in cognitive function, it takes quite a bit of time to do the protocol, but I am hoping I can work it in my life. It is especially good for chronic fatigue. I still have time to back out of sharing with my employer/doctor, but I think there is a reason I am back at this clinic. It takes a step of faith to share with people these intimate issues. What will they think? Will I be treated any differently? I know that there will be obstacles in caring what people think of me especially coming out with this book. I don't want it to reflect the scripture that says don't toss your pearls before swine. I always ask myself this question, is this how I want my story to end? I think right now, I am in a transitional phase, a healing phase, a timeout, so to speak.

I do know that no matter what I am going through, or the stress that is involved in my day, it is taking some quiet time to reflect, pray and seek God. I find Him refreshing and nurturing to my soul. I like to find ambiance images on the computer screen, whether it's a cabin by a lake with a thunderstorm or a night campfire, help me relax and meditate on God's promises. When I was at the fire station on shift, I would have a lot of downtime, some of it was nervousness for the next call, but it enabled me to spend quality time with Jesus. You can hear Him better with a quiet time out. I want to expect great news from Him, I want to see Him work through me and through others. Maybe this book is just one step or testimony to inspire another person struggling with mental illness to seek Him and know that He will work out all things to those who love Him. Romans 8:28 (NIV) states, *"And we know that in all things God works for the good of those who love him, who have been called according to his purpose."*

It's so hard when you are in the thick of a struggle. There seems to be no hope, no way out, day in and day out. You have succumbed to the same daily activities. But the seasons change, the sun will shine tomorrow, and God is a God of miracles. I had a patient recently

Chapter 9

who really was discouraged from struggling with his illness. There is no reason, no new discoveries as to why he was sick. Tons of doctors, tons of tests, still no answer. I am careful when I share about the Lord, I want to do it when God leads me and be appropriate in the work setting, but I really want to encourage him to do something for someone else. Serving others in this broken world nourishes your soul. There is so much brokenness that surely there is someone in a worse-off situation than yourself.

There was a time I thought I would never become a missionary, I always seemed to be focusing on another medication or how to go about daily activities, but the seasons change. God helped me get better. I was thinking recently of a time when I was single. I did a lot of eating by myself or going to the movies alone. I didn't want to miss out on new experiences because I was alone. I remembered going to a chicken pot pie diner and seeing an elderly man eating by himself. I took the chance and leading of the Holy Spirit and asked if I could join him. We had a pleasant dinner conversation together, and though I thought I was serving him, I think that experience was serving each other. I was lonely too, and stepping out to make another feel loved made me feel love as well. That's what I am talking about serving others. Our day can be too noisy, filled with chores, to-do lists, taking care of minor needs. But if we take a pause, a "selah" to hear God, that's when we can develop an intimate relationship with Him and be sensitive to His leading even if it's out of our comfort zone.

Sometimes when I am quiet and reflective, I can hear simple words God is sharing with me, an impression on my heart and mind. A lot of it is to relax. Relax in His spirit that He has all this thing called life figured out. He invites us to do His work because He loves us.

Chapter 10

"I have seen something else under the sun:
The race is not to the swift or the battle to the strong,
nor does food come to the wise or wealth to the brilliant
or favor to the learned; but time and chance happen to them all."

Ecclesiastes 9:11 (NIV)

This was the fight verse I had printed on my fight shorts during my pro fight. I heard it in a sermon once, the pastor talked about there is a right timing for everything, the right place at the right time or right opportunity. The wisdom about this is to discern when that is. I knew that my fighting opportunity was aligned just for me. I could feel it intuitively. I had scripture to back it up, I had opportunity, and I took it. It came with a lot of obstacles and adversity but ultimately, in victory and a moment I would never forget.

There has been a lot of changes lately. My father-in-law just had major heart surgery and is in the hospital, my uncle passed away, there are some changes in our church structure. The subject today was how to be guided by God and know when the right timing to make a major decision in your life. I sense I am on the merge of such a decision. I know I go through a lot of them, and I am always looking at how to grow and improve my life with the Lord and my walk. But the points that struck out of me were to obtain wisdom, obtain prayer, and your timetable may not be God's timetable.

Don't be too afraid to make those major decisions, but don't rush ahead either.

I have been thinking a lot about the timing of this book, how I am going to help others with mental illness, and how my story continues. Tomorrow is a big step in both my professional and personal health. I made an appointment with my doctor/employer to discuss some treatment plans available to me. I have worked for a medical clinic for more than two years off and on, I have never disclosed my personal medical information. I know my disability is covered under the ADA act, and I don't want to be afraid of losing my job. I want help, I want help with my cognitive function, chronic fatigue, and to develop more healthy habits. I do not know for sure what will go on tomorrow, but I feel from the Lord and talking with my husband that this is the right timing. If I need to cut back on some hours or try and get some brain boost treatments or NAD, now is the time to move forward.

James and I are also starting to go on a ten-day metabolic cleanse detox program, no alcohol, no sugar, or processed foods. We got a subscription to a wild Alaskan fish company for some fresh fish delivered to us, not farm-raised, and we get to enjoy salmon, halibut, and cod. I am looking forward to using this time as a fast to get closer to the Lord and have him direct our family. We see the importance of taking some accountability for our health, and instead of being dependent on alcohol, we need to figure out some alternative ways to cope with stress. I don't see us quitting wine for a long time but being healthier and more responsible as we encounter and place it in our lives.

Chapter 10

With my father-in-law in the hospital and my uncle passing, I have spent a little more time with family. I just can't stress enough the importance of developing your own relationship with God. Through all this life, major changes, major decisions, our salvation is the only thing that is assured. Today in our prayer, we surrendered our life to Jesus again, surrendering our own will to His and to place our desires in God's timing.

My stepdaughter is about to go through a major change in her life. She is entering high school. She has so many changes to face, and, reflecting on how my husband and I passed high school experience, we didn't make the best decisions. It was a critical time to surround yourself with the right friends, the right courses, the right activities. I want to encourage her to get plugged in and experience all she can. She is taking French for high school, and it made me think of when we took her to Spain and Paris. I felt that this trip would be a monumental moment for her, she actually may want to live in Paris, and we want to maybe retire in South France. We want to take French together as a family and encourage her on this dream.

Well, flash forward, and high school has begun. I have a lot of emotions to navigate being in a blended family. We are starting to hear the words on occasion, " I don't want to live with you anymore," " you never take me anywhere," " all we do is argue." Well, I can take responsibility for the arguing part, my husband and I are passionate people and can be a little loud with our emotions. I must try harder to communicate in more of a calm way, but that also means trusting God and my husband to be the leader of the home and let go of some of the control issues I have. My husband, as I have stated before, has PTSD and can have anger issues. My husband is strong, sexy, a leader but can have a temper, nothing that leads to violence but mostly manifests itself into both of us having extra cocktails, road rage, and some heated arguments. My husband's devotion to his family is the highest. He would do anything for his wife, children, and family.

I am excited to say my stepdaughter has decided to do something out of character for her. She joined the wrestling team! Wow, what a bonding experience we could have. We were having a parent Zoom meeting with the coach, and my husband shared that I am a former pro fighter. Proud a little, but for the most part, with being almost 80 lbs overweight from my former fighter days, how could I feel I could help her? I am still athletic with skills, but I started to feel defeated. I went into the gym the next day to do Muay Thai. I want to encourage her to go after what she wants. To hit the mats hard, and her work will be paid off. I must lead by example, and though the effort has been slow and steady, I am planning to take some experiences training together and to be there for her. I must find my purpose as a stepmother and back up the saying I have, which is to try things you have never done before because you never know where they may take you.

So, my conversation with my boss went well with sharing my mental illness, sometimes I think my coworkers suspect something going on medically, but I can't stop destiny from coming with the outcoming of my book and possible speaking engagements. I had a dream the other night of my hand being raised when I won the couture fight; what a feeling that was! I was on top of the world, and then I had a vision in my dream of my hands being raised when I was standing in front of thousands again, sick with my bipolar, standing in front of a church congregation, catatonic. This was at my worst. Embarrassed, humiliating, people moving away from me fearful. Thank God they just let me be and didn't interrupt the service. How did I experience the top of life to the bottom of life? It's kind of strange how bipolar extreme highs and extreme lows are. I know, like Peter in the Bible, how to be abased and how to abound. I think it comes down to the message I want to truly convey. You are worthy. God loves you and accepts you how you are. You don't need to have that hand raised for victory or in defeat. In a dog-eat-dog world, we can sit in the calmness of the morning and know that there is a God who would do anything for you, a God that died on the cross for you. My success now is a little different. I have always wanted to continue to help people and encourage them to be the best they can be despite any setbacks, illnesses, or negative experiences. But I know my worth is in loving others with the love I have received. The forgiveness I have received I can now extend to others. My goals are to be a loving wife, stepmother, daughter, and sister. To share this love with others and not worry what they will think about you. I love the quote: "Sometimes courage is not a roar, sometimes courage is at the end of the day saying I will try harder tomorrow."

I believe God's right opportunity and timing are coming for our family. It may be for James and me to start getting serious about veterans and mental health, a subject we both can team up and join in God's work together. We just need to take time to spend some quiet time with the Lord. God's answers are not in the loud wind or shatters of an earthquake but in a quiet whisper. I don't want my life to be so loud to miss that discerning voice of God that says, go this way, take this turn, speak to this person. We need to stay close to the word, to community, and to the quiet time to hear Him. It's hard navigating all these emotions in life. But one thing I want to end with is to know that you are worthy. Worthy of love, forgiveness, respect, and to experience all that God has for you on this earth.

I am just about to publish this book and wanted to share a little bit about my mother-in-law Ada Dilley. She had recently passed away, and yes, it was during the Christmas season. I somewhat can't help but think there is an amazing Christmas party in heaven that God wanted her to go to. I have had several family members and my puppy Scout, who passed away during this season. As I briefly mentioned earlier in my book, she suffered from bipolar disorder. I have been slowly coming out of the dark and sharing my secret, and last month when we were visiting her to obtain legal guardianship, I shared with her my condition and that we both had the diagnosis. She felt sorry for me, and I vowed to take care of her as best as my husband and I could. I sometimes get nervous about what it will be like when I am older and what my mental status will be? Who will come to visit? Where will I be? I believe she was meant to be my mother-in-law; I have faith that the Lord will care for me and bring someone like me into my life just as He did for her. I know now she is pain-free, with clear thoughts, joyful, and dancing with Jesus. I

Chapter 10

wanted to also dedicate this book to her memory and celebrate those who struggle with mental health, that a piece of our legacy will live on to encourage and bring hope to others.

About the Author

Kimberly Rose has been a fighter all her life. She is a former professional MMA fighter, 2008 bronze medalist with USA national championships for amateur boxing, and a Muay Thai enthusiast. As a paramedic for twenty-three years, she has fought to save the lives of countless patients, and she has shared the gospel throughout the world, going on several mission trips to Mexico, Africa, Cambodia, and Thailand. But perhaps her biggest fight is the one she has daily with herself, being diagnosed with mental health issues in 2010. With the help of her faith and the loving support of her husband, family, and two pit bulls, Milo and Nova, Kimberly works every day to promote health and wisdom.

CPSIA information can be obtained
at www.ICGtesting.com
Printed in the USA
LVHW081820220622
721890LV00011B/284